ASPECTS OF BARNSLEY 7

DISCOVERING LOCAL HISTORY

Edited by

Brian Elliott

Wharncliffe Books

First Published in 2002 by
Wharncliffe Books
an imprint of
Pen and Sword Books Limited,
47 Church Street, Barnsley,
South Yorkshire. S70 2AS

For up-to-date information on other titles produced under the
Wharncliffe imprint, please telephone or write to:

> **Wharncliffe Books**
> **FREEPOST**
> **47 Church Street**
> **Barnsley**
> **South Yorkshire S70 2BR**
> **Telephone (24 hours): 01226 - 734555**

ISBN: 1-903425-24-7

A CIP catalogue record of this book is available from the
British Library

Cover illustration: *Demolishing the old obelisk at the end of Church Street, 1932*
   (Norman Ellis Collection)
Illustration, contents page: *Tramcar No. 10 passes Mason's drinking fountain,*
   Sheffield Road, c.1912 (Norman Ellis Collection)

Printed in the United Kingdom by
CPI UK

CONTENTS

INTRODUCTION

by

Brian Elliott

Welcome to the seventh book in the *Aspects of Barnsley* series. Once again, our contributors (seven of them new) have written and compiled an interesting and varied collection of articles, produced at a time when a great deal of 'rethinking' is taking place about the future of our historic town. For some people, the word 'historic' may seem an odd appellation for a place such as Barnsley but the considerable volume of work which has now accumulated, some eighty articles, does much to document and celebrate the history of our town and neighbourhood.

Regular contributor Melvyn Jones opens the present volume with a most appropriate and fascinating subject, exploring the ancient place-names of Barnsley's Metropolitan Borough. Mel rightly says that our area 'rings with the names of history', skilfully taking us through some 2,000 years of name-giving, explaining origins and the evolution of many local places. The editor's chapter on medieval Barnsley offers some insights into a somewhat neglected area, making use of on the ground evidence, maps, aerial photographs and some new documentary sources.

Well-written autobiographical and reminiscence pieces are always welcome additions to the series and this volume contains several excellent examples. Roy Portman describes his working life at one of Barnsley's former engineering works: Needhams, once world-famous for making colliery pulley wheels. The article is enhanced by some of Roy's superb photographs. Many of us will remember the taxi rank that once stood at the approach to the Exchange Railway Station and adjacent to Barnsley Bus Station. Mike Stringer, writing from Billericay, Essex, not only describes his father's taxi business but also writes evocatively about his own early life in Barnsley during the 1950s. Colin Taylor is an even more distant writer, living in the USA, and his affectionate memoir relating to family, places and events in Smithies and Barnsley, set mainly during the inter-war period, is extremely clear.

Margaret Mann provides us with interesting descriptions of Canon

Sorby and several characters and personalities of old Darfield whilst Barry Jackson's exploration of pre-1960s Monk Bretton is based on a recorded interview with one of its most colourful village characters: Mr Johnny Weston. I will never forget chatting to Johnny about the history of Monk Bretton when I was a teenager. He showed me around the village, pointing out and explaining many historic features, and then we went to his garden where, under an old pear tree, he told stories and anecdotes about the village and its characters, and of course talked a great deal about his love of cricket. Barry has produced a superb tribute and a most interesting description of an old Monk Bretton that has unfortunately just about disappeared.

John Goodchild continues to support the *Aspects* series, using source material from his unique Local History Study Centre at Wakefield. For this volume we benefit from John's well-known interest in coal mining history. His essay on the Edmunds and Swaithe Main collieries, based on an even more detailed research paper, provides new material concerning that busy industrial area to the south of the town. John's short piece on schoolmaster Charles Ward of Darton Grammar School, also reminds us of the Victorian practice of presenting illuminated addresses to individuals in recognition of service and achievement.

In the same genre as diaries, school log books are a fascinating source of information, relating to both personal and official life. What makes John Broom's selections from the Royston Secondary School log books so special is that they relate to the formative years of the school during the 1930s and continue into the difficult war-time period. There are of course many former pupils who will find John's meticulous research of considerable interest. When I began teaching at the school in the early 1970s one of the most experienced staff was Mr Arthur Wilson who, apart from war service, had taught at the school since its foundation in 1934.

Norman Ellis began collecting postcards more than thirty years ago and has carried out a great deal of research and writing, due to his interest in subjects and themes such as transport, collieries and West Riding towns and villages. It is very pleasing to receive a contribution from him on Barnsley, illustrated with some wonderful photographic images from his extensive collection.

Transport, albeit short-lived, is the subject of Richard Buckley's essay on the Dearne District Light Railways. Using original source material from Sheffield Archives, he helps us to appreciate some of the complexities and indeed the eventual demise of (apart from modern developments) the last complete tramway opened in the UK.

Wharncliffe Books, an imprint of Pen & Sword Books, continue to be generous in commissioning the Barnsley volumes and also for helping me develop the entire series which now extends to more than twenty UK locations and about thirty-five titles. Recent or forthcoming new *Aspects of...* areas include Teesside, Lancaster, Calderdale, North Lincolnshire and Chesterfield. Many thanks are due to Charles Hewitt and his small team at the Drill Hall, Eastgate – Barbara, Paula, Rachael, Sylvia, Paul, Roni, Jon, Mattie, Michelle, Jonathan and Kate – for their continued encouragement, advice and hard work. Lastly and by no means least, my sincere thanks to all the contributors and to all our loyal readers.

1. WHAT'S IN A NAME?
THE ANCIENT PLACE-NAMES OF BARNSLEY METROPOLITAN BOROUGH

by Melvyn Jones

THE BARNSLEY AREA rings with the names of history – the River Dove, Barnsley itself, Dodworth, Darfield, Grimethorpe, Elsecar, Gunthwaite, Cheapside, West Gate (in Monk Bretton) Blucher Street, Peel Street – names covering at least 2,000 years of name-giving in the area covered by the metropolitan borough. And the tradition has continued in more recent times with residential expansion, but this time just to confuse us we now have whole estates such as the Athersley South estate full of names from the Peak District such as Bamford Avenue, Buxton Road and Peveril Crescent and Athersley North full of names from Nottinghamshire such as Beeston Square, Bramcote Avenue, Laxton Road.

This chapter is concerned with the old names of Barnsley Metropolitan Borough, names that were in place at least 700 years ago. This includes the names of every town or village in the metropolitan borough and almost all the hamlets and farms.

Sources

It is important to say something about sources of information. The first serious modern work on the place-names of South Yorkshire was Armitage Goodall's *Place-Names of South-West Yorkshire* published in 1913. Following an historical introduction the book consists of an alphabetical listing of the main place-names of the area, giving early spellings and suggested meanings. The next major contribution was Ian Maxwell's chapter 'The Age of Settlement' in the volume entitled *Sheffield and Its Region* published to accompany the British Association for the Advancement of Science's meeting in Sheffield in 1956. Written by a geographer and containing a series of interesting distribution maps, the study looked at the phasing of settlement in the Anglo-Saxon and Viking periods in an area centred on Sheffield and extending into Derbyshire, Nottinghamshire and Lincolnshire. This was followed in 1961 by A H Smith's volume for the English Place-Name Society on the *Place-Names of the West Riding of Yorkshire* dealing with the wapentakes of Strafforth and Staincross. Although

it was published before a number of important studies were written
that questioned certain long-held beliefs about the chronology of
Anglo-Saxon settlement and the nature of Danish Viking settlement
in eastern England, Smith's volume remains the major source for
understanding the meaning of South Yorkshire's place-names. It is
the main source for this chapter.

Since Smith's volume was published two names have dominated
English place-name studies: Margaret Gelling and Kenneth
Cameron and their published works have been important sources for
this study. Margaret Gelling was appointed as a research assistant to
the English Place-Name Society in 1946 and by 1992 had risen to be
President of the society. She is the author of the English Place-Name
Society's volumes on Oxfordshire and Berkshire and co-author of the
volume on Shropshire. She is also author of *Signposts to the Past*
(1978) and *Place-Names in the Landscape* (1984). Kenneth Cameron,
was Professor of English Language at the University of Nottingham
from 1963-87 and died in 2001. He wrote the three-volume *The
Place-Names of Derbyshire* in 1959 and was working on the seventh
volume of *The Place-Names of Lincolnshire* at the time of his death.
His *English Place-Names*, first published in 1961 was completely
revised and re-published in 1996. He is also the author of important
studies of Celtic and Viking settlement and place-names.

The formation of place-names
Most place-names are made up of different parts called 'elements'.
Some, however, are composed of just one element such as Haigh
and such names are called **simplex** names. Most names are
complex consisting of two or more elements such as in Barns / ley,
Cud / worth or Ing / birch / worth. Where a name has two elements
the first one is called the **prefix** and the second one the **suffix**.
Additionally, some place-names have an **affix**, an additional word to
distinguish one settlement from another as in Little and Great
Houghton and High Hoyland and Hoyland Swaine.

Celtic place-names
Celtic or British, of which Cornish and Welsh are descendants, is the
language that was spoken by the people of England from an
unspecified point in the late prehistoric period (the oldest source
being *c*.325 BC), through the Roman period (from the mid-first
century until the early fifth century AD), until it was gradually
ousted by Old English, the language spoken by the Anglo-Saxons. In
the Roman period the Barnsley area was a backwater area and there

Figure 1. Market day at Penistone early last century. Penistone was first recorded in the Domesday Book in 1086 as *Pengestone* and *Pengeston*. Before the construction of the purpose-built cattle market in 1910, Penistone's beast market was held in the main streets of the town. *Chris Sharp, 'Old Barnsley'*

are no Roman names.

Not surprisingly either, only a few Celtic place-names have survived. The oldest names in the area are almost certainly the river names – the Dearne, the Don and the Dove. The meaning of Dearne is unknown. Don, which also appears in Russia and is the first element of the Danube, is believed to be a Celtic word for water. The word Dove is definitely Celtic and means 'the black one'.

The prefix in the name Penistone (Figure 1) is also believed to be Celtic as is Penisall, the name of a place at Langsett that occurs in documents between the twelfth and fourteenth centuries but which no longer exists. The Celtic element *penno* means a ridge, in this case the long ridge between the valleys of the Don and the Little Don, with Penistone lying at the foot of its northern slope and Penisall on its southern slope. Penistone means the farmstead or village (Old English *–tun*) by the ridge and Penisall means the hollow (Old English *–halh*) on the side of the ridge.

That a British population existed in South Yorkshire when the Anglo-Saxons entered is testified by the Anglo-Saxon names that have survived referring to the Celtic population and their settlements. These include Cumberworth, just across the boundary of Barnsley Metropolitan Borough in Kirklees. The prefix in Cumberworth is Old English *cumbre,* a borrowed Celtic word which in modern Welsh is *Cymro,* 'Welshman'. Cumberworth is therefore the 'enclosure of the Welshmen'. Similarly, the Old English *walh* means foreigner, Briton or Welshman and this has survived in the village of Wales eight miles east of Sheffield. Another British word that occurs in two South Yorkshire place-names is *egles,* which is itself borrowed from the Latin *ecclesia.* It means church and is presumed to refer to the presence of a Christian church acknowledged by the then heathen Anglo-Saxons. The word occurs in the place-names Ecclesfield (treeless stretch of country containing a British church) and Ecclesall (nook of land containing a British church). Finally, it used to be believed that Bretton, as in Monk Bretton, meant farm or village of the Britons, and this is the derivation given in Goodall (1913) and Smith (1961). However, in the fourth edition of Eilert Ekwall's *Dictionary of English Place-Names* published in 1966 the author suggests that the derivation is not a reference to Britons but means newly cultivated farm or village. Furthermore, Bretton as a name referring to a Celtic population is not discussed at all in Gelling (1997) or Cameron (1996).

Anglo-Saxon place-names

The Anglo-Saxons were settlers who colonised the lowland parts of eastern and southern Britain after the departure of the Romans in *c.*AD 410. They were Germanic tribespeople who came from the coastlands of north-western Europe from the lower reaches of the River Rhine to River Elbe and into southern Jutland. It is believed that the people who settled in South Yorkshire were Anglians from southern Jutland. They gradually settled in the Celtic kingdom of Elmet, of which the Barnsley area was part, from the early seventh century and their presence is reflected in the many names of Old English origin in the Barnsley area – Old English being the general name given to the dialects of the Germanic language spoken by the Anglo-Saxons.

The Old English and Viking place-names (see below) in the Barnsley area can be divided into two main types: habitative names and topographical names. Habitative names have as their main element a word meaning settlement – farm, hamlet, village, town, estate or enclosure. Topographical names have as their main element a word referring to the physical setting of a place – such as hill, valley or woodland clearing.

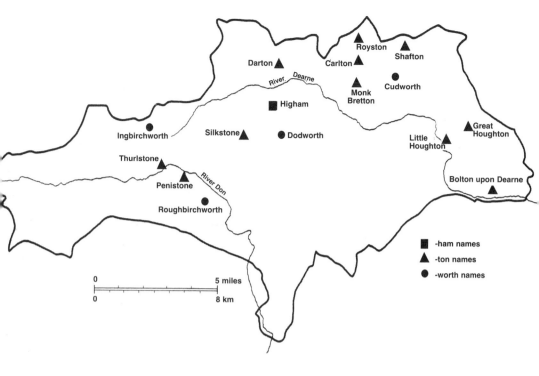

Figure 2. Old English *-ham*, *-ton* and *-worth* names within the boundaries of Barnsley Metropolitan Borough.

The most common Old English habitative names are *-ham* (homestead), *-tun* (now usually spelt *-ton* and meaning farm, village or estate) and *-worth* (enclosed settlement). The distribution of names containing these elements in the Barnsley area is shown in Figure 2. There are only two *-ham* names in the Domesday Book of 1086 from the whole of South Yorkshire – Rotherham and Bilham. This is perhaps not surprising as *-ham* was the most commonly used habitative name at the beginning of the Anglo-Saxon period, and as has already been pointed out the penetration of Angles into South Yorkshire did not take place until the early seventh century, more than 250 years after the first settlements in the coastal areas of eastern England. There is one *-ham* name in the Barnsley area, Higham (high homestead), which was first recorded in 1271.

There are eleven surviving *–tun* settlements, including Penistone and Monk Bretton already noted above. The others are Bolton upon Dearne, Carlton, Darton, Great and Little Houghton, Royston, Shafton, Silkstone and Thurlstone. The villages of Royston, Silkstone and Thurlstone all have a personal name as a prefix which could either be the founder or a manorial overlord: Hror's tun, Sigelac's tun and Thurulf's tun. Thurulf in Thurlstone is a Danish Viking personal name, making Thurlstone a Scandinavian hybrid name (see below). Bolton means a farm or estate with its buildings, Carlton is the farm or village of the churls or freemen, Darton is the deer *tun* (park or enclosure?), the Houghtons are the farms or villages in the nook of land (*halh* = nook) and Shafton means the farm or village made of poles or marked by a pole.

There are also four -*worth* settlements in the Barnsley area: Cudworth, Dodworth, Ingbirchworth and Roughbirchworth. The villages of Cudworth and Dodworth both have personal names as prefixes: Cuda's enclosure and Dod's enclosure, while Ingbirchworth and Roughbirchworth both mean birch enclosure with the additional affix of *eng* (Old Norse for meadow) and 'rough' to distinguish between the two places.

The most common Old English topographical place-name element in England is -*leah* meaning woodland clearing, and it is very common in the Barnsley area occurring no less than eighteen times and testifying to the well-wooded landscape at the time (Figure 3). As with the habitative names, a number of the -*leah* names have as their first element an Anglo-Saxon personal name, for example, Eored's clearing (Ardsley), Aethered's clearing (Athersley), Beorn's clearing (Barnsley), Cubba's clearing (Cubley), and Thancred's

Figure 3. Old English -*field* and -*ley* names within the boundaries of Barnsley Metropolitan Borough.

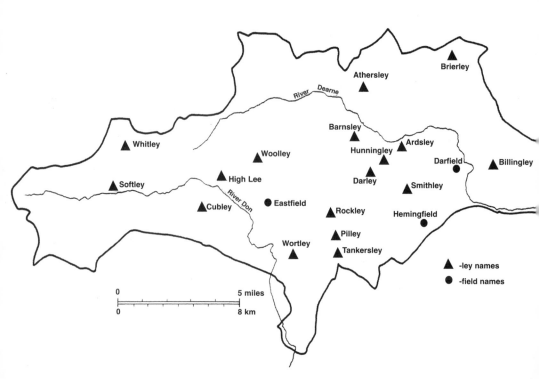

Figure 4. Tankersley church. Tankersley was recorded in the Domesday Book in 1086 as *Tancresleia* (Thancred's clearing). It was also one of the fifteen places in South Yorkshire in 1086 that had a church (and a priest).
Chris Sharp, 'Old Barnsley'

clearing (Tankersley, Figure 4). The name Billingley is particularly interesting because of the *-ing* element in the middle of the name which may be from the Old English word *–ingas* meaning 'people of' or 'dependents of', which would mean that Billingley means the clearing of Billa's people or dependents. Hunningley, near Ardsley may have the same derivation (the clearing of Hund's people).

The first element in two of the *-leah* names tells of the vegetation in the woodland clearing: Brierley (briar clearing) and Bromley (broom clearing); in three others about their wildlife: Darley (clearing frequented by deer) and Rockley (clearing frequented by rooks) and Woolley Manor Farm at Silkstone (Woolley meaning clearing frequented by wolves); and in another what was being grown in the clearing: Wortley (vegetable clearing).

The element *-feld*, meaning a stretch of treeless country or heath in an otherwise well-wooded area, is also a common Old English place-name element but it only occurs three times in the Barnsley area, in Darfield (treeless country frequented by deer), Hemingfield (probably treeless country of Hymel's people), and Eastfield at Thurgoland (not mentioned for the first time till the relatively late date of 1562). Two other Old English place-name elements to do with woods and their clearance are *-hyrst* (wooded hill), as in Upper Elmhirst, and *-rod* (clearing), usually spelt *royd*, as in High Royd Farm at Hoyland Swaine and Royd Moor Farm at Thurlstone.

In the western and central parts of the area there are several names which refer to the hilly nature of the landscape. These include Barugh from the Old English *beorg* (hill), Gawber (*galga beorg*, gallows hill), Hunshelf meaning Hun's *scelf* (shelving terrain) and Langsett (long hillside). The name Wharncliffe means *cweorn clif*, referring to the fact that along the rocky edge overlooking the Don valley there was an important quern industry. Querns were hand-operated grindstones for converting cereal grains into flour. On-site evidence suggests that the 'factory' at the foot of the crags may have had its origins in the Bronze Age and that it was still active in the medieval period.

There are also three separate places in the Barnsley area named after the spur of a hill (Old English *hoh-*) on which they are located: High Hoyland, Hoyland Nether (with its nearby hamlet of Upper Hoyland) and Hoyland Swaine (Figure 5). It is assumed that the substitution of *hoy-* for *hoh-* represents a reflection of local dialect as in the local pronunciation of coal (coil) and coat (coit). Swaine in Hoyland Swaine was the name of a medieval manorial lord, Swane de Hoiland having been recorded as witnessing a deed in the late twelfth century.

There are also a number of places which include the element *-denu*, meaning a long, narrow, curving valley. Most of these are in the extreme west on the Millstone Grit moors such as Harden (hare valley), Windleden (windswept valley), Dearden (deer valley) and Swinden (swine valley) but the name also occurs much further east at Worsbrough in the Dove valley at Lewden (sheltered sunny valley).

Figure 5. Hoyland Swaine and its surrounding landscape. The place was simply recorded as *Holan* and *Holande* in the Domesday Book of 1086 but by the thirteenth century had acquired the suffix Swaine, being recorded in 1266 as *Holandswayne* and in 1379 as *Holand Swayne*. It lies at over 850ft above sea level, high above the upper Don valley. *Chris Sharp, 'Old Barnsley'*

Lastly, there is a substantial number of places along the Dearne and Dove valleys, which contain the place-name element brough or borough: Sprotbrough; Conisbrough, Mexborough, Barnburgh, Worsbrough, Stainborough, Measborough and Kexbrough, the last four being within the boundaries of Barnsley Metropolitan Borough. The suffix is from the Old English *burh* meaning a fortified or defended place. Worsbrough means Wirc's fortification, Stainborough means stone fortification, Measborough as in Measborough Dike means boundary fortification and Kexbrough probably means Kept's fortification. When the forts were built is a mystery; they may be of prehistoric origin or they may have been constructed by the Celtic peoples of Elmet to stop the incoming Anglo-Saxons or they may be of Anglo-Saxon origin.

It used to be thought that the habitative names were the earliest Anglo-Saxon names, but Margaret Gelling has written persuasively that topographical names are possibly the earliest names given to places in England by Anglo-Saxon settlers. She quotes examples of places whose names are known to have been changed from their original topographical ones to habitative ones. Unfortunately, no documents earlier than the Domesday Book of 1086 exist for South Yorkshire so that it is not possible to test Gelling's ideas in the Barnsley area.

Viking place-names

The word 'Viking' was the name given by the Anglo-Saxons to the raiders from Scandinavia in the late eighth and ninth centuries. The name probably originated from 'Viken' the name for the area around Oslo Fiord in Norway but it soon became a synonym for pirate or raider and plunderer. The Vikings who came to Britain came from Norway and Denmark. The Norwegians eventually settled in the Shetland and Orkney islands, the Hebrides, the west coast of Scotland, the Isle of Man, the east coast of Ireland and north-west England. The Danes eventually settled in eastern England between the Tweed and the Thames.

The Viking age is said to have begun in 793 when the monastery of Lindisfarne was raided. The raiding continued in the first half of the ninth century and then in 865 a great Danish army arrived in England under the leadership of Halfdan, who conquered the Anglo-Saxon kingdom of Northumbria, the whole of East Anglia and the eastern half of the midland kingdom of Mercia. Northumbria stretched along the eastern side of the Pennines from the Tweed to the Humber and included the Barnsley area. After gaining their military victories the Danish army was joined by agricultural settlers, although there is still debate about how big the agricultural settlement was. Like previous colonists to Britain the Danes settled here because of population pressure in their homelands. The Danes had settled permanently in Yorkshire by 875. Soon after 886 a treaty between the Danes and King Alfred, Saxon king of Wessex, formally recognised the area ruled by the Danes, called *Danelaw*, which included all the territory north and east of Watling Street (the modern A5) which ran from London to Chester.

The Barnsley area was therefore within Danelaw where the impact of the Danish population, their institutions and language was great. The Danish settlers must have entered South Yorkshire via the lower reaches of the Don and Trent and then up the valleys of the Don and its tributaries the Dearne and Rother. They re-named villages and farms, established new settlements, imposed their administrative systems and introduced many new words into the evolving language of the region's inhabitants, including many of the dialect words that are still used today, e.g., *addle* (to earn), *gawp* (to stare), *laik* (to play) and *teem* (to pour).

The Danish Viking place-names in England come in three forms. Either they are completely (the prefix and suffix) in Old Norse, the language spoken by the Danes; or they are a combination of Old Norse and Old English (what are known as hybrid names); or they contain Scandinavianised elements (either prefix or suffix, or both) of Old English words, either because the Danes could not or preferred not to pronounce the Old English word.

The most common Scandinavian place-name element in Yorkshire as a whole is *-by*. There are 210 *-by* place-names recorded in the Domesday Book of 1086 in Yorkshire with another 69 first recorded in post-Domesday medieval records. When used by the Danes it meant town or village. The term is still used today in the word *by-law*, meaning a local law. There are ten places in South Yorkshire containing this place-name element but all but one are in the eastern part of the county including five – Barnby Dun, Scawsby, Balby, Cadeby and Denaby – beside the River Don, a major colonisation route. The one *–by* place-name in the western part of the county is in the Barnsley area, and that is Barnby, in Barnby Hall and Barnby Green near Cawthorne (Figure 6). A manor on or near the site of Barnby Hall was recorded in the Domesday Book in 1086 as *Barnebi*. This is a wholly Scandinavian name, the prefix being the Old Norse personal name *Bjarni*, so the name means Bjarni's farmstead or village.

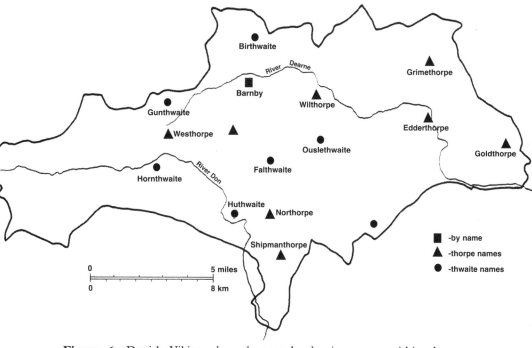

Figure 6. Danish Viking *-by*, *-thorp* and *-thwaite* names within the boundaries of Barnsley Metropolitan Borough.

The second most common Danish Viking place-name element in South Yorkshire is *-thorp*. It occurs 17 times on the 1:50,000 Ordnance Survey maps that cover South Yorkshire and there is almost a dozen 'lost' settlements (i.e., settlements whose names appear in old documents but which do not exist any more on the ground) that contained the *-thorp* element. It means an outlying farm or hamlet dependent on a larger, earlier settlement. There are seven surviving *-thorp* settlements in the Barnsley area: Edderthorpe, Goldthorpe, Grimethorpe, Noblethorpe, Northorpe, Westhorpe and Wilthorpe (Figure 6). In addition, Shipmanthorpe, in Wortley parish, occurs on early Ordnance Survey maps but not on modern ones, the buildings having been demolished. Edderthorpe, a hamlet to the north of Darfield, is a hybrid name, first recorded in 1208 as *Edricthorp*, the prefix being the Old English personal name Eadric. Goldthorpe and Grimethorpe also have personal names as the first element: Goldthorpe is Golda's outlying farm or hamlet and Grimethorpe is Grim's outlying farm or hamlet. Golda is, like Eadric, an Old English name, but Grim is an Old Norse one, so that Goldthorpe is another hybrid name but Grimethorpe is a purely Scandinavian name. Wilthorpe is another hybrid name meaning wild or desolate outlying farm or hamlet, as are Northorpe, north of Wortley (north outlying farm or hamlet), and Westhorpe, west of Hoyland Swaine (west outlying farm or hamlet). The lost *-thorp* settlement in Wortley parish, Shipmanthorpe, probably means shepherd's outlying farm or hamlet (Middle English *schepman* = shepherd).

The third most common Danish Viking place-name element in South Yorkshire is *thveit* (thwaite) (see Figure 6), and there are seven surviving examples in the Barnsley area: Alderthwaite in Hoyland Nether (Alfward's clearing), Birthwaite at Kexborough (birch clearing), Gunthwaite (Gunhild's clearing), Falthwaite at Stainborough (clearing broken up for cultivation), Hornthwaite at Thurlstone (wild boar clearing), Huthwaite at Thurgoland (Hugh's clearing), Ouslethwaite at Stainborough (blackbird clearing, Figure 7). Birthwaite, Gunthwaite and Hornthwaite are all purely Scandinavian names, the others are hybrid, having an Old English prefix.

There are a number of other wholly Scandinavian names in the Barnsley area besides Barnby and some of the *-thorpe* and *-thwaite* names already mentioned. These include Thurnscoe (*thyrne skogr*, thorny wood), Schole Hill at Penistone (*skali*, sheds, temporary buildings), and Staincross (*steinn kross*, stone cross).

Figure 7. Ouslethwaite Hall. Ouslethwaite, which means 'blackbird clearing', was first recorded in 1382 as *Osilthwayt*. It is one of a number of place-names in the Barnsley area which contain the names of animals. Others include Hornthwaite (wild boar clearing), Woolley (clearing frequented by wolves), Darfield (open stretch of country frequented by deer), Rockley (clearing frequented by rooks) and Harden (hare valley). *Brian Elliott*

OUSLETHWAITE.

Then there are the Scandinavianised names where the Old Norse speakers substituted the Old Norse element for the Old English. This occurs, for example, in the name Stainborough (stone fortification) where the Old English *stan* has been replaced by the Old Norse *steinn*. The Danes also substituted *c* for *ch* as in Carlton and Carlecotes (at Thurlstone) which would originally have been Charlton (homestead of the churls or freemen) and Charlecotes (cottages of the churls or freemen).

In addition to these town, village, hamlet and farm names there are the names of fields and lanes and other minor places that have survived that show the Old Norse language was once used throughout the area. *Kjarr* (marsh), for example, survives throughout the area as a field name and in the settlement names of Elsecar and Blacker Hill. *Holmr*, meaning an island in a marsh, is also found in the area at Holmes between Great Houghton and Thurnscoe. The use of *eng*, usually spelt as *ing*, was widespread in river valleys and means damp meadow land. Every village in the Dearne valley had its ings and Wombwell Ings, Billingley Ings and Bolton Ings are still named on modern Ordnance Survey maps. Another minor Old Norse name is *hlatha* (barn) as in Laith Croft at Dodworth, Laithes Lane at Athersley and Low Laithes between Ardsley and Darfield. There are also two Old Norse words for a wood that survive: *storth* as in Storrs Wood between Cudworth and Darfield and Storrs Wood and Upper and Lower Storrs between Hoyland Swaine and Oxspring; and *lundr* (a small grove) as in Lundwood and Lundhill (Wombwell).

Although occurring in rural villages, as in West Gate at Monk Bretton, the Old Norse word *gata*, now spelt 'gate', meaning, lane or street, is a Viking word most associated with urban areas. Barnsley has its Eastgate, Westgate and Church Street used to be Kirkgate, kirk (*kirkja*) being the Old Norse word for church. The word gate was also introduced into the mining industry at an early date for the main underground roadway in a colliery (the main gate).

The Vikings also gave their names to several old administrative divisions in South Yorkshire. Barnsley Metropolitan Borough is, of course, part of the former West Riding of Yorkshire, riding being the Danish Viking name (*thrithungr*) for a third part. At a more local level, counties were divided into smaller units for judicial and administrative purposes. Outside Danelaw, groups of parishes were known as *hundreds*, but inside Danelaw they were known as *wapentakes*. It is believed that wapentake denoted a meeting at which agreement was shown by brandishing weapons. South Yorkshire was divided into three wapentakes: Lower Strafforth, Upper Strafforth and Staincross. Strafforth wapentake is presumed to take its name from a meeting place at Strafford Sands in Mexborough where there was a major crossing of the River Don. The Staincross wapentake is named after its meeting place, the former hamlet of Staincross, where presumably a stone cross stood.

Conclusion

It is often said that the British landscape is many-layered and it has been likened to a *palimpsest*, that is a piece of parchment which has been written on, then the writing removed and written on again, the process being repeated on a number of occasions. Each time the odd word, letter or curl from previous writings persist on the parchment. This is certainly true of place-names in the landscape. In the Barnsley area, Celtic, Anglo-Saxon and Danish Viking names have been successively introduced, but many have come and gone, leaving a real mixture of names in any given locality.

And the names discussed here tell only half the story. Names have continued to be given since the Middle Ages up to the present day, particularly the names of streets and lanes and public houses – e.g., Boggard Lane at Penistone, Shambles Street, Cheapside, Blucher Street and Peel Street in central Barnsley, California Gardens at Worsbrough Common, St Helens Avenue in Smithies, Reform Row at Elsecar, the *Wharncliffe Arms*, the *Lord Nelson* and even *Durty O Dwyers* – all have a tale to tell – but that will have to be on another occasion.

Bibliography

Cameron, K, *English Place-Names*, Batsford, revised edition, 1996.
Ekwall, E, *The Concise Oxford Dictionary of English Place-Names*, fourth edition, Oxford University Press, 1966.
Gelling, M, 'Topographical settlement-names', *The Local Historian*, 12, No.6, 1977, 273-77.
Gelling, M, *Signposts to the Past: Place-names and the History of England*, third edition, Phillimore, 1997.
Gelling, M, 'The Present State of English Place-name Studies', *The Local Historian,* 22, No. 3, 1992, 114-27.
Goodall, A, *Place-Names of South-West Yorkshire*, Cambridge University Press, 1913.
Maxwell, I 'The Age of Settlement' in D L Linton (ed), *Sheffield and Its Region*, British Association for the Advancement of Science, 1956, pp. 121-37.
Smith, A H, *The Place-Names of the West Riding of Yorkshire, Part I, Lower & Upper Strafforth and Staincross Wapentakes*, English Place-Name Society, Volume XXX, Cambridge University Press, 1961.

2. GLIMPSES OF MEDIEVAL BARNSLEY

by Brian Elliott

ON THE MORNING OF SATURDAY 11 May 2002, whilst walking on Cheapside, I was handed a glossy A4 leaflet on *Rethinking Barnsley*. It concerned the on-going planning weekend held at the Falcon Centre in which John Thompson & Partners were facilitating a 'hands-on' and 'open process' which would include teams of residents and representatives from a variety of organisations and where anyone could 'drop-in' and have a say on Barnsley's future. We were also promised 'stimulating glimpses into the future' via the premiere of the film *Rethinking Barnsley – The Film*. For several weeks, in fact since the news broke in the *Barnsley Chronicle* on 28 March (headline: 'Touch of Tuscany for Town') and 5 April (headline: 'Future is halo in the sky'), Will Alsop's ideas of a new Barnsley attracted national media attention. On Saturday 6 April, for example, Martin Wainwright in *The Guardian* described the Stirling Prizewinner, among other things as 'the main promoter' of the 'Tuscan alternative' whose 'vision on the motorway' of 'slender towers rising from an encircling, inhabited town wall, a Santa Maria di Barnsli above the foaming river Dearnini' also gained the support of the council's executive director David Kennedy who acknowledged the 'wow factor' of Will's Urbino dreams. All credit to Yorkshire Forward's interpretation of the government's 2000 Urban White Paper, selecting Barnsley as one of their six 'Renaissance towns' and paying for the ideas of internationally acclaimed architectural practices. With £150 million from Europe in the background, their sketches could become real, hence the commendable consultation process: after all, agreement is far better than imposition. There are of course huge social and commercial advantages in creating and promoting a 'good-looking town'.

Massive changes have taken place to urban Barnsley during the last fifty years. Many buildings of historic and architectural interest have been lost and key traditional areas such as the old market place, May Day Green and Churchfields transformed under the aegis of virtually imposed redevelopment schemes, totally ignoring how much such areas were valued by local people, former inhabitants and visitors. Thankfully, despite waves of what I can only describe as 'official vandalism', the distinctive Barnsley character remains intact and in recent years there has been a Renaissance of writing and art from people still fond of their native town. And, as Will and his colleagues have rightly said, there remains much to celebrate.

Back in the twelfth and thirteenth centuries a small number of people who did not even live in our area were involved in a process of rethinking Barnsley. Their Christian thoughts and plans had unashamedly commercial motives. The individual or corporate decision, sanctioned via international headquarters in France, was for the building of a new town on a new site. But the change, though radical, took many years to achieve, stretching over several generations and through a long period of medieval recession. Analysis of the 1379 poll tax returns suggests that as late as the end of the fourteenth century Barnsley was about the same size as Hemsworth and only slightly larger than the neighbouring villages of Wortley, Worsbrough, Cawthorne and Cudworth (Figure 1).

Figure 1. Top Twenty Settlements in the Wapentake of Staincross in 1379

Place	Married couples	Single persons	Sons and daughters	Servants	Rank
Hemsworth	59	17	8	6	1
Barnsley	58	21	1	6	2
Wortley	46	16	9	1	3
Worsbrough	40	20	6	11	4
Cawthorne	40	17	14	4	4
Cudworth	41	10	3	3	6
Monk Bretton	26	14	2	0	7
Ardsley	25	14	5	2	8
Dodworth	19	20	10	4	8
South Hiendley	25	12	10	9	10
Brierley	23	11	0	0	11
Notton	23	4	2	1	12
Thurlstone	23	4	5	1	12
Darton	19	6	2	1	14
Silkstone	16	9	6	2	14
Tankersley	16	9	8	4	14
Shafton	18	6	3	4	17
Wintersett	21	2	0	1	18
Woolley	13	9	6	11	19
Hunshelf	18	3	3	2	20
Thurgoland	14	7	4	0	20

Even the granting of a market charter was no guarantee of economic success. Markets at places such as Braithwell, Hooton Pagnell and Campsall never took off or fell into decay as did Tickhill's. Even the

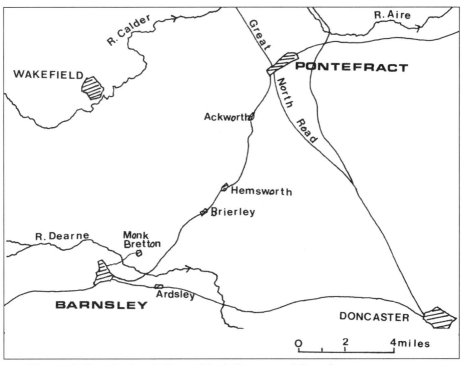

Figure 2. Barnsley in relation to Monk Bretton and Pontefract.

great city of York suffered economic stagnation.

Barnsley's fortunes began to change after the Norman Conquest when the town came under the absentee control of the Cluniac priory of St John at Pontefract, located about twelve miles eastwards (Figure 2). A smaller sister priory ('Monk Bretton'), soon to fall out with its French owners, had developed at a pleasant location in the Dearne valley near the Lundwood, much closer to Barnsley (Figure 3). The

Figure 3. Barnsley and Monk Bretton Priory.

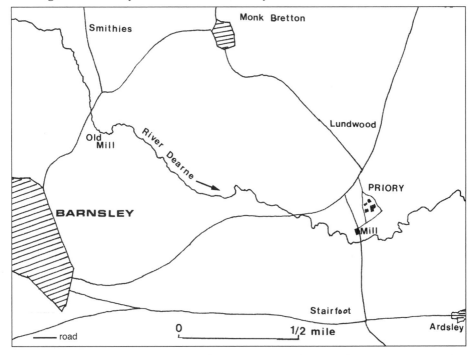

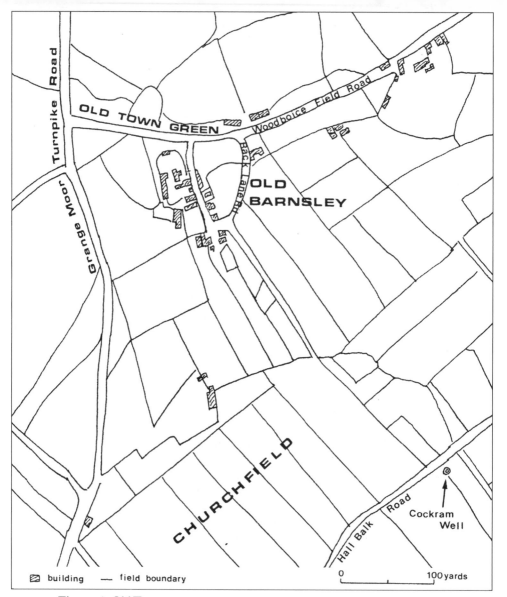

Figure 4. Old Town.

small group of brothers here were also to have a significant impact on the evolving town, pioneering new enterprises such as coal mining, iron-making and textiles, and using the waters of the river as a power-source for processing raw materials. Place-names such as Old Mill and Smithies owe their survival to sixteenth and seventeenth century economic activity and associated problems (there were numerous legal disputes) in areas well known by their monastic predecessors.

The original Saxon hill-top settlement (Figure 4) was eventually superseded in favour of a planned new town strategically sited less than a mile to the south where communications were far better. A characteristic street pattern was laid out, centred on a broad market place. In 1249 the Pontefract monks obtained a charter from Henry III for a weekly Wednesday market and an annual four-day October fair. By Tudor times the monks enjoyed the ownership of the manor of Barnsley and its court, the markets and fairs, demesne and woodland and the township tithes, along with the adjacent township of Dodworth. By 1544, as we can see by reference to Figure 5, analysis of a subsidy roll now shows a significant difference in size between the developing market town of Barnsley and nearby communities.

Figure 5. Top Twenty Settlements in the Wapentake of Staincross in 1544

Settlement	Persons assessed	Rank
Barnsley	86	1
Worsbrough	32	2
Hemsworth	30	3
Cawthorne	30	3
Brierley	29	5
Cudworth	28	6
Thurlstone	27	7
Wortley	25	8
Monk Bretton	23	9
Thurgoland	22	10
Wintersett	21	11
Clayton	20	12
Carlton	19	13
Dodworth	17	14
Hunshelf	17	14
Notton	17	14
Woolley	17	14
Royston	15	18
Langsett	14	19
Tankersley	14	19

As early as 1280 the primary settlement was already being referred to as Old Town or Old Barnsley. But it was not abandoned. It continued to support a number of craftsmen and farmers; indeed a few key families such as the Rookes, Oxleys and Chappells were to enjoy economic success during the seventeenth century and yeoman farmer John Littlewood, who died aged just twenty-nine in 1693 left a substantial inventory of goods and chattels. Two 'guest beds' were recorded for Old Town in an official government survey of 1686 (cf 64 in Barnsley itself). Thus, Old Town was not a quiet backwater but

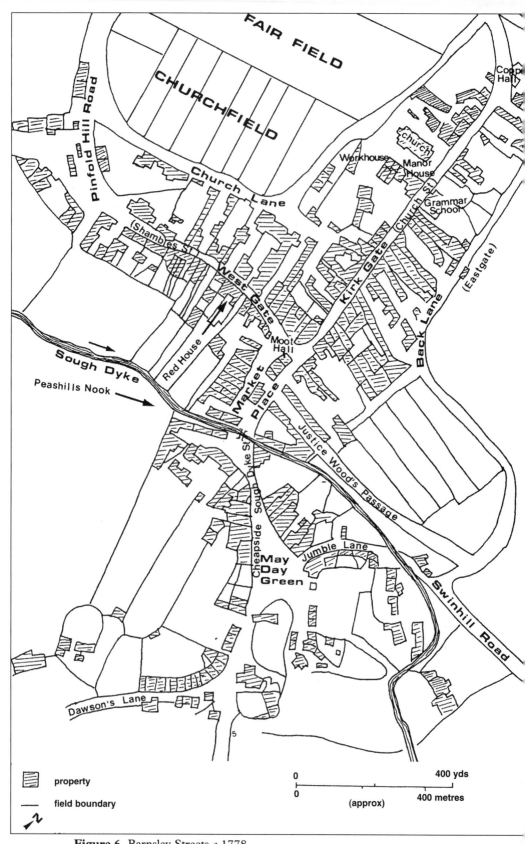

Figure 6. Barnsley Streets *c.*1778.

like other associate hamlets such as Pogmoor and Gawber, had a number of key families.

The main elements of the new medieval town of Barnsley are evident in Fairbank's survey of 1777-78 (Figure 6). The market was a central feature, carefully sited along a hill, making full use of the Sough Dyke, the small westerly-flowing stream which, as its name suggests, served as the town drain. A small timber bridge crossed the Dyke, giving access to a roughly triangular open-space called May Day Green. By this time the Green's periphery had been encroached by small cottages and wiremakers' workshops. It extended through Cheapside towards Jumble Lane and Dawson Lane at the edge of the common. The adjacent Swin(e)hill or 'Swithin' area, like the Green, was used on market and fair days for livestock sales.

Radiating from the top of Market Hill were the two principal town streets: Westgate (Shambles Street) and Kirkgate (Church Street). St Mary's Church and the Manor House occupied commanding positions on Kirkgate, a little away from the hub of the market, near the northern limits of the town. Behind the church, a chapel of ease of Silkstone parish, lay the large open-space known as Fairfield, a natural arena for the annual fairs and festivals.

The two main thoroughfares were each linked by roughly parallel back lanes (Church Lane and Back Lane, later called Eastgate) and the spaces between the lanes and streets were filled with a mix of the backs of shops, inns, workshops, small courts, gardens and orchards. The numerous courts and yards, many hidden from street view may also have served, despite regulation, as unofficial and opportunistic trading points, meeting places and even compounds for produce. Although the location and fabric of dwellings and outbuildings was renewed and supplanted, the form of settlement here probably changed very little from medieval times through to the nineteenth century.

Modern oblique aerial photographs can be used to good effect to further delineate the medieval town. The first example (Figure 7), from the 1950s, prior to large-scale town re-development, shows that medieval elements are clearly visible, Fairfield in particular being an easily distinguishable feature. The view is also useful because of the distant vistas of countryside to the south and west which would have had to be crossed via the Race Common road which cut across Barnsley Moor.

A 1960s aerial view (Figure 8) shows the town centre before the major development of May Day Green. The basic layout of the old streets are apparent although Shambles Street has been widened and

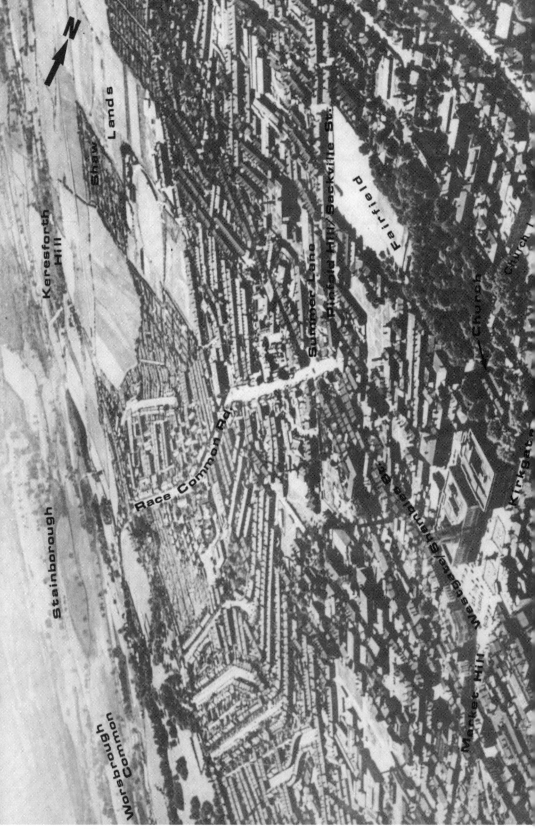

Figure 7. Oblique aerial view *c.*1955.

Figure 8. Oblique aerial view *c.*1965.

Figure 9. Gawber Hall during demolition.

Church Street is now dominated by substantial public buildings such as the Town Hall and College.

The discovery in 1999 of medieval timbers during the development of the former Butterfield's store and the recent work at 41-43 Church Street (Ashley Jackson's art shop) owned by the *Barnsley Chronicle* serve as tantalising reminders that timber-framed structures were once quite common. Though a little out of the town, Gawber Hall, an exceptionally fine gabled house, demolished in the 1930s, had what appears from photographic evidence to be very fine quality timber features (Figure 9). The more recent (*c.*1962) removal (and destruction) of a substantial tithe barn of five bays, located near

Figure 10. The medieval tithe barn.

to the town centre, serves as a spectacular demonstration of the use of timber in another high status building (Figure 10).

A parliamentary survey of Barnsley dating from 1649 is a very interesting source of information on local buildings many of which

HOUSE MUNICIPAL BUILDINGS, BARNSLEY.

Figure 11. The Manor House.

would have evolved on medieval sites. Details are given of some forty properties, ranging from the Manor House to derelict cottages. The Manor House (Figure 11) is described as 'a capital messuage... an ancient strong timber house... consisting of a spacious Hall, two parlours, two other nether rooms with a buttery, 3 lodging chambers [at the south end of the property]...kitchen, a parlour, a diary house with two chambers over them [at the north end]...'. Nearby was a substantial seven-bay barn, stable, various outhouses, a garden, courtyard and a bowling green. All structures (bar some of the outbuildings) were 'in good repair' and 'not fitt to be demolished' and, most interestingly, the materials would be of little value anyway since 'wood stone and slate was very plentiful'. 'Quarries of stone and slate [were situated] in and upon the waste or comon', suggesting a convenient source of building materials still available.

The survey also makes reference to six small cottages (one in a ruinous state) which were part of an endowment for the chantry chapel of St Mary's church. They appear to have been of two bays, with a modest outbuilding, probably a stable/barn or 'shop' (workshop) and were worth small annual rents of a few shillings. A further nineteen town 'cottages' are itemised, with approximate sizes given and the names of present and previous occupants. These were almost certainly of a higher status, some serving a commercial or dual purpose function. It is likely that most of them were located in the market place and on the main town streets. Elizabeth Baxter's property (formerly occupied by Will Garnet), probably a shop and dwelling had three bays and was 'lately repaired'. Another is described as 'two cottages under one roof four bays a shop lately made into a dwelling' showing a recent change in usage. Terms used to describe the cottages included 'an ancient building', 'a strong handsome building' and 'strongly built near the market place'. Many of them appear to have been divided into several habitations. We also have a glimpse of overcrowding and poverty, one property described as 'ruinous' but 'divided into 4 habitations [for] four families of very poor people.' Evidence from early wills certainly supports multiple family occupation in many Barnsley town properties, especially on Kirkgate, Westgate and in the market area.

Many Barnsley deeds were registered at Wakefield from the early eighteenth century. Some of the properties that are described are likely to have been of late-medieval origin. They also provide us with valuable information about the developing professional and commercial heart of the town. A deed of 1710, for example, includes reference to an inn known as the *Sign of the Cross* which had barns and outbuildings and gardens in the possession of Ann Addy, Joseph Crofts, Joseph Ashforth and William Thompson. In 1712 a deed relating to George Usher, apothecary (of Barnsley) and John Meager (of Old Barnsley, gentleman) concerns two shops 'standing in the market place...with chambers over and cellars under...'. Another old inn, known as the *Boot and Shoe* was located on Kirkgate, under the occupation of Josia Hawksworth. Cottages are also mentioned on Pinfold Hill, off Westgate. An ancient Kirkgate property, 'commonly called or known as Folly Hall', occurs in 1711. We also learn of the *Black Bull Inn*, Kirkgate, held by Cornelius Wood in 1716. There are many other interesting examples, referring to town shops and workshops.

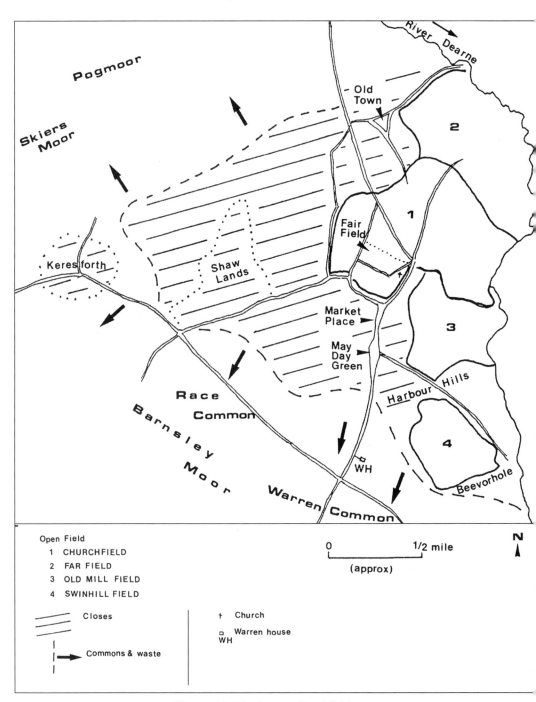

Figure 12. The late-medieval field pattern.

Between 1703 and 1756 Barnsley deeds make references to 2 Esquires, 37 gentlemen, 16 yeomen, 2 husbandmen, 1 servant and 1 labourer. From the professional class there are 4 attorneys, 2 parsons, 2 schoolmasters and 8 apothecaries. Commercial and craft occupations dominate: mercers/drapers (20), grocers (4), hardwaremen (2), tobacconists (1), chandlers (3), booksellers (1), bakers (3), butchers (7), chapmen (2), innkeepers (12), clockmakers (3), carpenters/joiners (3), weavers (4), feltmakers/hatters (5), ropers (2), tanners (4), curriers (2), saddlers (2), cordwainers (2), fellmongers (1), buttoners (1), masons (2), plumbers/glaziers (3), wiremakers (6), nailors (1), and blacksmiths (4).

Most of the families living in and around the town had some farming interests. The 1649 manorial survey states that in Barnsley there are 'four town fields... called Churchfield, Old Mill Field and Swinhill Field...'. These ancient fields are frequently mentioned in medieval and later deeds. Their locations and approximate form can be identified from a series of maps produced by William Fairbank and a township map of *c.*1775 (Figures 12-13). The fields are arranged in a north-south line, occupying most of the lower land towards the Dearne valley. The alignment of the medieval strips

Figure 13. The field pattern in the township area *c.*1778.

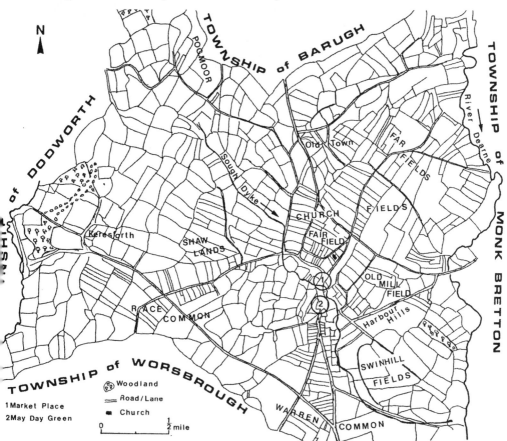

N

1 Market Place
2 May Day Green

Woodland
Road/Lane
Church

0   ½ mile

shows that in the main they followed the easterly descending slopes. Churchfield occupied the largest area, in the centre of the township and also contained the ancient trading site of Fairfield.

The common to the west and south of the town was said to be 'large' but there was no 'chase' or wood 'worth valuing'. Between the common and wastes were numerous 'ancient enclosures'. Field-names such as Horse Fair Shutt, Beast Fair Shutt, Cockpit Close and Peashills are of medieval origin. The ancient field system appears to have been easily identified, despite many years of inclosing and renting of land in each area. The immediate post-enclosure landscape can be seen in Figure 13. The entire township area has been inclosed but the medieval area, stretching from Old Town towards the Shaw Lands and across to May Day Green towards the Dearne can be seen by reference to the small irregular closes and the inclosed strips of the former open fields.

Figure 14. The magnificent timber-framed interior of 41-43 Church Street. Tree-ring analysis suggests that the structure was built in or shortly after the spring of 1463-64. The late medieval building would have been a high status dwelling judging by its quality interior, and possibly occupied by a wealthy mercer or draper because of its prime trading location. It is the oldest most complete secular building in Barnsley. The discovery of a jetton coin, placed there by the original builders/owners supports the scientific dating. Restoration work, funded by the *Barnsley Chronicle*, with help from English Heritage and Barnsley MDC, was completed in August 2002.

Sources

This article is based on information from Part One of the author's M Phil thesis 'Barnsley: the Anatomy of a Yorkshire Market Town and its Neighbourhood, c.1660-c.1760' (University of Sheffield, 1990), where full references are given. Copies are lodged in Barnsley Archives and Local Studies and in the University of Sheffield Library.

3. MEMORIES OF MY WORKING LIFE AT NEEDHAM AND BROWN'S OF BARNSLEY

by Roy Portman

ON LEAVING MARK STREET CENTRAL SCHOOL, aged fourteen, where my favourite subject was Woodwork, I sought work at various carpenters, joiners, cabinet makers and even undertakers, but to no avail. Jobs were hard to find in 1937 and for a time I was out of work and attended what was then known as the Junior Instruction Centre in Racecommon Road. My father suggested that I go down to Needham & Brown's in Pontefract Road and ask to see Charlie Needham, whom my father knew. The interview resulted in the offer of a job, as an apprentice engineer's pattern maker, working in wood. I started work in October, 1937.

Needham's was an iron and brass foundry and engineering works with much of the work for local collieries. The speciality was making haulage winding engines, pit cages, head-gear pulleys, centrifugal pumps for pit washeries etc. In those days many of the pits still used steam driven winders, and one of the items often needing replacement were cylinder covers as they tended to crack under pressure. Very often, these were urgent jobs, treated as 'break down' which meant working overtime. Under private ownership very few pits had spares ready for emergencies, so the foundry worked all night on many occasions to complete a job in the fastest possible time.

At this point in my story, some background information about the history of 'Needham's' may be of interest. The business was well-established in Barnsley. John Needham, a moulder, moved from Sheffield to Barnsley in the early 1860s. By 1870 he had entered into a partnership with Edward Hall, John Qualter and George Bower, each putting up the sum of £100. Later, the company name was changed from 'The Railway Foundry' to 'Needham, Qualter Hall & Company.' Initially, premise space was leased under four railway arches in Midland Street, from 1867 to 1928. In 1880 expansion also took place, on an acre of land behind the arches. Five years earlier John Needham had died, his company shares reverting to the remaining partners; but from the sale his sons rented space from Qualter Halls until 1877 by which time the firm was generally known

Figure 1. Needham Brothers & Brown Ltd, engineers, Pontefract Road, Barnsley, 1972. *Roy Portman*

as Needham Bros & Brown. About this time NB&B appears to have moved into Pontefract Road, adopting the old premises of the Barnsley Gas Works, the new gas works having moved to Old Mill in 1870 (Figures 1-2).

Figure 2. Needham Brothers' engineering works, Pontefract Road, July 1976. On the right, a storage compound was made after terrace houses were pulled down. *Roy Portman*

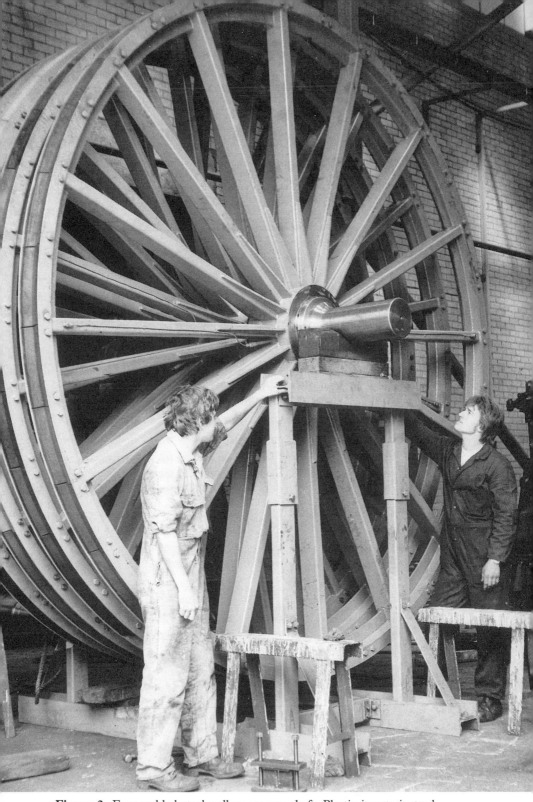

Figure 3. Four welded steel pulleys on one shaft. Plastic inserts in trod. Made at Needham Brothers, for Abercynon Colliery. *Roy Portman*

In my early days Needham's manufactured cast iron pipes of all shapes and sizes for the pits and chemical plants. Pipes in the pit washeries had to take a mixture of coal and water called slurry; this ground away the wall of the pipe until it was paper-thin, eventually breaking through. The pit engineers would try and patch it up as a temporary repair until we could make a replacement. I remember on one occasion, myself and a work mate going to one of the pits about 7 pm, after doing our usual day's work, to make a template for a pipe. We then went back to Needham's and worked through the night, making a skeleton pattern from the template. The moulders were then able to cast a new pipe the following day.

One of the biggest jobs was head gear pulleys, made in various diameters, from 10ft to 20ft (Figure 3). The largest pulleys took up a great deal of space in the Moulding Shop. They were cast from two 5-ton ladles, one carried by each of the shops' cranes. Transporting these pulleys had its problems and a police escort was needed to get them to their destination by road. Eventually, the large pulleys were made in halves, making both the transporting and fitting a lot easier. One half of a 12ft pulley I made pattern equipment for now stands on the site of Wharncliffe Woodmoor (1, 2 & 3) Colliery, Laithes Lane, a monument to those men who were killed in the disaster of 1936 (Figure 4) .

Figure 4. Roy Portman, retired pattern-maker, with the pulley he helped to make at Needham Bros, now a memorial on the old Wharncliffe Woodmoor site.

Figure 5a. Turning pattern for a 5ft pulley. The timber is built up in segments layer by layer to complete the pattern. The shelves above hold hundreds of tooth core boxes for spur, bevel and double helical wheels.

Figure 5b. Pattern-maker Roy Portman in the old pattern shop at Needham Bros, Pontefract Road, Barnsley.

I liked working on both pulleys and pump patterns: there was a lot of wood carving and everything had to be very accurate (Figure 5a and 5b). Pattern-making is a highly skilled craft. I attended 'night school' for three evenings a week, learning engineering drawing, moulding practice, and theory and practical pattern-making. It wasn't easy for an apprentice to make the grade. Many youngsters gave up their apprenticeship and left to get money in the pits and elsewhere. Apprentices had, of course, to put up with a lot of leg-pulling when they first started. A favourite was to send them to the other side of the firm to borrow a 'sky-hook'. Sometimes they even

Figure 6. The new Pattern Shop converted from timber and pattern store. The original shop had been part of Barnsley's first Gas Works, as was the Moulding Shop. *Roy Portman*

came back with it in a barrow, a lifting hook, complete with about a hundredweight of chain! There were a few good lads but after apprenticeship most left for better jobs with more pay.

There were many characters during my time at work, with nicknames such as 'Tiger', 'Trigger', 'Chip-pan', 'Rubber-legs' and many more. Some of them were born funny men, though sometimes the recipients of their wit did not think so, such as the labourer who asked a Director,

'When a tha having thee holidays this year?'

'Why do you want to know?' asked the Director.

'Well', came the reply, 'It wouldn't do for thee and me to be off the same week would it? Ar would they manage wi 'art us?'

On another occasion two mates were talking about Christmas. 'I'm going to buy myself the Guinness Book of Records', said one. 'What for?' said the other, 'You haven't got a gramophone.'

Another incident was when a labourer-cum-handyman was set on to put a new pane of glass in a window. After finishing, he picked up his ladder, turned round and put the end of the ladder straight through the new glass he had just put in. Another character was one of the blacksmiths who would cut your hair in the dinner hour. You had to sit on an anvil for this, on a bit of old sacking. I don't know if he had a fixed charge for this service or you just gave him what you thought it was worth!

As already mentioned, Needhams took over the old gasworks (Figure 6). What had been the old retort house became the moulding shop. The pattern shop had also been part of the gas works (Figure 7).

Figure 7. To the left of the Goods Entrance is the old frontage of the one time *Fisherman's Rest* which closed in 1907. *Roy Portman*

Figure 8. This photograph was taken in the old Pattern Shop *c.*1966. It is presentation of a wrist watch to George Needham, retiring foreman moulder. Robert Needham, company Chairman and Managing Director is handing over the watch. To George's left (suited) is Laurence Needham, another Director. The two workers sat next to Laurence Needham are Horace Hall (a moulder) and 'Billy' Goodhall. Just to the left of the stove pipe is Harry Needham (wearing cap, without glasses) who was foreman patternmaker. Roy Portman is just in view, standing, wearing a cap, shirt and tie, on the right of the group.

Needham's expanded and eventually took over an old beer house called the *Fisherman's Rest* which closed in 1907 (Figure 8). This became part of the blacksmith's shop. One of the older employees, a moulder called Harry Newsome, used to talk of having a pint at the *Fisherman's Rest* in his younger days.

One of the regular events was the firm's annual trip, whereby the men decided on the destination and Needham's paid for the transport. One year it was to Blackpool by a special train shared with the Ceag Works outing. The first trip that I went on was in 1938, to the British Empire Exhibition in Glasgow. We left Barnsley on Friday night by special train arriving in the Scottish city early Saturday morning. The whole day was spent at the exhibition and in Glasgow. This included a look at the new liner, *Queen Elizabeth*, still on the Clydeside slips before being launched later that year. Travelling back through the night we arrived back in Barnsley on Sunday morning, tired out. That outing was talked about for a long time, the day trip that almost became a weekend! There were other trips, but in 1957 not many were interested in the idea. The trip was cancelled and the workforce accepted fifteen shillings (75p) instead. Ten years later, in 1967, the trip 'allowance' was still fifteen shillings!

Here is a short explanation, without being too technical, about the actual job of pattern-making. Before any job can be cast in iron, a replica of the item has to be made of wood. Canadian Yellow Pine is used as it is soft and easy to work. However, it must be seasoned timber, free from knots and shakes. The pattern-maker works from scale drawings, a drawing of the finished article, not of the pattern which may look entirely different. The reason is, allowance must be made for machining and any large holes or cavities have to be cored out, needing a separate core box. The pattern will often be split or jointed to enable it to be drawn from the moulding sand. The pattern-maker must know moulding techniques and machining practices.

A pattern-maker needs specialised tools: long paring chisels, gouges and so, all expensive items, and you had to buy your own tools when I started in the trade. I had a bit of luck. An Uncle, who worked at Newton Chambers, bought a set of tools from a retired pattern-maker as he wanted a hand-brace and a set of bits. My father then bought the box of tools from Uncle Jack, less the brace and bits. So, this gave me a good start, and over the years other tools were bought and added to the box. One item was a good set of wood turning gouges. These came in handy as I had many patterns to turn during the coming years.

As a lad, one of my regular jobs was making gratebar patterns. These were mainly for pit boilers. However, I have also made gratebar patterns for Albert Hirst, a bakery down Hayes Croft. If they could not send a spare bar, someone had to go and get the size when the baking oven fire was out. A sought after job, as it usually meant a free pork pie!

Much later, an apprentice got a tools allowance during the first three years. The apprentice ordered tools up to a figure agreed between the union and the management, usually from a traveller who visited the works on a regular basis, the firm footing the bill.

After the opening of the new market complex in the mid-1970s, Needham's became the centre of controversy with letters in the local press about the black cloud that came over the market every afternoon about 3 o'clock. This was the time the furnace blower was switched on. The firm received many complaints from market traders and inspectors, but, Needham's argued, they had been there a lot

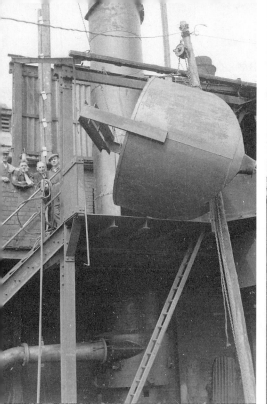

Figures 9 & 10. Erecting a new furnace in August 1953. *Roy Portman*

longer than the new market (Figures 9-10), so not much else could be done about it at the time. Perhaps the outcome would have been different now with the environmental laws of today.

Working for a small firm, you are asked to do all sorts of jobs. I have fitted locks, repaired doors, windows and office furniture. I have done roof repairs and replaced woodwork on overhead cranes and other plant. I have also done jobs for all the Directors, both on and off the premises. Enough to say, my efforts (e.g., taking quality photographs of the haulage gear etc) saved them a lot of money on professional fees.

Throughout my working life I have had to put up with a lot of noise, mainly from the saws and other machinery of the Pattern Shop and a large compressor housed nearby. For various reasons it was impossible to use ear-muffs. Before I was forty I started to loose my hearing, and later I got the awful ringing in the ears as Tinnitus developed. I have had a number of minor operations but to no avail. I became increasingly frustrated with all the noise, which led to a number of long spells off work. In the end I was assessed as 'unfit for work' by the DHSS and placed on invalidity benefit. I remained on the books at Needham's until I was sixty-five for any benefit that may

Figure 11. Dismantling furnace after closure of foundry section, Needham Bros, November 1984. *Roy Portman*

accrue to me.

My last ten years of service was as Foreman, checking the work of others in both the pattern and moulding shops. I was supposed to be on the staff, but there was no staff pension for me, no golden handshake, no parting gift, not even a retirement clock. All I did receive was a cheque for my entitlement under a scheme that management paid into for a one-off payment at sixty-five, the biggest benefit from which was for injury or death. This was the so-called pension scheme.

In the early eighties Needham's foundry interests were closed down (Figure 11). In 1984 the patterns held in stock were sent to the bonfire at Locke Park. In the afternoon, looking on as the fire was prepared, I recognised many

Figure 12. Roy Portman: self portrait, 1970.

Figure 13. Snap-time, foundry yard.
Roy Portman

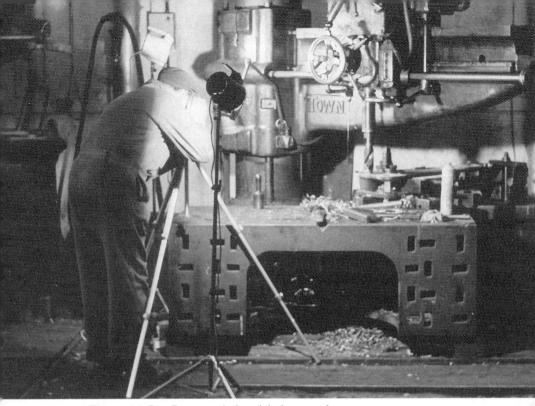

Figure 14. Roy Portman: industrial photographer.

Figure 15. The yard at Needham Bros: machinery ready for the auction.

pieces I had made during my working life. That evening, the Mayor, Councillor Don Baines, lit the bonfire and set fire to my life's work. My efforts for the firm over forty-three years gone up in smoke!

Now I am no longer working I can devote more time to my lifelong hobby of photography (Figures 12-15) and to a more recent interest, local history. Time now seems to go much quicker than when I was working.

Random notes from Needham's records

After the closure of Needham's, in June 1994, I was invited by John Hislop, then Barnsley MBC's Conservation Officer, to tour the works with him as he had been given permission to take some photographs of the workshops before the sale of machinery etc. He knew that I had been employed there and would be able to give him some information about the works. As it turned out, we had a guided tour by John Rouse who had been in charge of the Machine Shop. He was a lathe operator and had been retained by the receivers until the machines had been sold, so he could tell John Hislop facts about the machine shops. The area where I had worked had changed since the foundry section had closed in 1984 and what had been the pattern shop where I worked now contained screw cutting machines. The former moulding shop with its two bays was now an erecting shop, mainly for hydraulic equipment.

The lighting was poor, it being a dull day but we were able to get some pictures. One of the things we saw was part of an unfinished funicular railway, destined for Malaysia. The winch was complete but not the inclined carriage.

Barnsley Archives contacted the receivers to see if they could get any of the company records. They managed to collect three large cardboard boxes of material, including old order books. What follows is a few notes that I later made in the archives, using some of the records:

March, 1960. Mr W Wilkinson, former director pensioned off with £6 per week.

December 1966. Bills for whiskey, rum, gin and one green Chartreuse, also lists of gifts to managers and engineers at pits, from 1916-1919. Records of cash gifts to staff. I remember having to make small wood cases for some of the bottles just before Christmas, over a number of years. I also recall, though not shown in the records, a tradition of me boxing up an Albert Hirst pork pie, a gift from Charles Needham to his sister in Cumbria.

In one box were four Barclays Bank books for employees holiday accumulation fund, 1944-67.

In the 1970-80 wages book I found details of my take-home pay. On October 24 1980 it was £65.74 (£83.36 at top of the note) but no record of hours worked. When I married, in 1955, my take-home pay was £9.10s.

In 1968 Harry Needham retired and I became foreman pattern-maker and now got a Christmas present of £10.

Items: 1891, an 18ft pulley for South Kirkby Colliery cost £39.9s. Contract price was £66.12s. Total weight of pulley: 3 tons 6 cwts. 1969: A 10ft dia pulley for Geevor Tin Mine, Cornwall, with shaft and phospher bronze bearings, total cost, £1,083.

I worked on that pulley and at a later date, when on holiday in Cornwall, visited the mine's surface workings and saw the pulley at work.

4. Stringer's Station Taxis: Memories of a Small Family Business in Barnsley During the 1950s and Early 1960s

by Mike Stringer

ANYONE FAMILIAR WITH Barnsley in the 1950s and 1960s will remember the taxi rank at the approach to Exchange Station, near to the bus station (Figures 1a & 1b). The proprietor was my father, John or 'Jack' Stringer who started his business there in 1950. He had not always been in the taxi trade but had always preferred to be self-employed. Like many others, his working life started as a miner in the Jump area where he was born.

Figure 1(a). A Station Taxi business card. *M Stringer*

Figure 1(b). This view of the old Barnsley Bus Station, taken from the railway bridge, probably dates from the late 1950s/early 1960s. Part of the Exchange Station Approach can be seen on the left of the photograph. The Stringer Taxi cabin is out of shot but part of a parked taxi is just visible. *H Copley*

Tel. Barnsley 4634

STATION TAXI'S
Exchange Station Approach, Barnsley

Prop:- J. B. STRINGER
49, Chapel Street, Ardsley
Barnsley, Tel. 3980

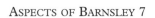

Figure 2. Grandma Stringer (my father's mother) with her dog 'Betty' outside her cottage at Skiers Spring, Hoyland, where I was born.

Not satisfied with life as a miner in the 1930s, and in his twenties, Jack travelled down to the more prosperous London and South East England, to try and find a new life for himself and my mother. Although with no previous experience, he managed to find work as a scaffolder, quickly becoming promoted to Foreman. By the late 1930s my sister was born and they had now bought a new 'semi' in Dagenham. But along came the war and because of the bombing and constant living in and out of air-raid shelters my mother was advised by her doctor to return to Barnsley, as by this time she was pregnant, expecting me. The house in Dagenham was sold and in 1940 I was born at my grandmother's cottage at Skiers Spring, Hoyland (Figure 2). We had to stay with various relations, including my mother's old family home at 26 Newton Street, Barnsley.

My parents bought a house, number 20 Princess Street, but it was a struggle for them to make a new start in Barnsley. All their furniture and possessions which they had placed in storage on selling their Dagenham property had been looted during an air raid. The new house had to be furnished with old, second-hand furniture, new furniture being very scarce and expensive. I remember growing up amongst all this Victorian and antique furniture, of little value then but worth a fortune today. Like most people then, we did not have a bathroom. Bath-time was once a week in a galvanised tub in front of the living room fire. The toilet was situated at the bottom of the garden.

Father began to earn a living at home, making leather goods such as handbags, purses and wallets; and also table and bedside lamps. My mother helped him with this work. Mother's health was not good, my infant brother having died, and she was seriously ill with a heart condition. Consumer goods were in very short supply and they were always able to sell their home-made items to private customers who would call at the house. I always remember the smell of leather and the rattle of his leather-working treadle machine up in the attic. Unfortunately, he fell foul of the Inland Revenue and could no longer afford to carry on with the work. At this time he tried to start a business with a former Barnsley football player, making, bottling and selling their own brand of household bleach which they called 'Wimso', obviously plagiarising the famous brand 'Wimsol' which older readers might remember. The venture was not successful.

Jack always enjoyed owning his own transport, having since the early 1930s had a motorbike and sidecar. We often went out for day trips in the sidecar, me sat on my mother's knee and my sister in the back, squashed into the little boot seat. By the mid-1940s he had graduated to a little Austin Seven. I remember days out in this little car, going into the countryside around Barnsley, for picnics. As he was one of the few car owners around at the time he often had requests from local people to take them on journeys to see friends or relations, for which he received payment. From this modest beginning, he got the idea to start a full-time taxi service from home, so having sold the Austin Seven, he bought a larger car. Petrol was in short supply but as he was now in business he managed to get permission to buy the extra petrol he needed. He had a telephone installed in the house and before long trade was so good that he bought a second car and employed part-time drivers, Don, Phil and Henry, working from our house during the evenings, trade being very slack during the day (Figures 3-4).

By 1949 father decided to expand his business and start a taxi rank in the town centre, the Exchange Station Approach being the obvious place. He was aware that there were other taxi firms interested in the site, so had to be quick in applying for permission.

Figure 3. Jack Stringer with one of his first taxis, outside 20 Princess Street, late 1940s. *M Stringer*

Figure 4. One of Jack Stringer's first taxis, parked in his yard at 20 Princess Street, Barnsley. Late 1940s. *M Stringer*

British Railways approved his application on condition that he provided a full-time taxi service at the station during the day.

At Princess Street he rented a garage and he set to work building in sections the future taxi cabin. I was nine years old at the time and helped as best I could, passing tools etc to him. He told me that on completion of the job he would reward me with anything I wanted. I had my eye on a boxed set of Britain's lead zoo animals which were displayed in the window of Town End Stores, sadly demolished in the early 1990s. Although my parents had on a previous Christmas bought me a whole wooden toy farmyard, complete with lead animals, my mother on this occasion decided that I was too old for such toys, so I was reluctantly persuaded to have a collection of second-hand woodworking tools instead, as they were more useful! I was very disappointed and never took to carpentry.

At this time I attended Agnes Road Junior School (Figure 5), our headmaster being Mr Frudd or 'old Fruddy'. In common with most other boys at the school I had on occasions to visit his study for a caning, but never got to dislike him. He was a jovial man, although fairly strict, always prepared to share a joke with the kids and make fun of himself – even referring to his wooden leg.

It is easy to become nostalgic about one's childhood but I really do believe that at the time Barnsley was a marvellous place for a child to grow-up in. There was little traffic in the town compared to today and there was always somewhere to go and something to do. Playing whip and top up and down the street, hop-scotch, collecting car numbers, playing up the backs, coming home from school with pockets full of marbles and collecting cigarette cards. Like other kids I collected as many as I could by swopping but I was fortunate in that occasionally my father would call into a little newsagent's shop in Sheffield when he was over that way and bring back a complete set for me, which would have cost about half a crown (12.5p). As well as

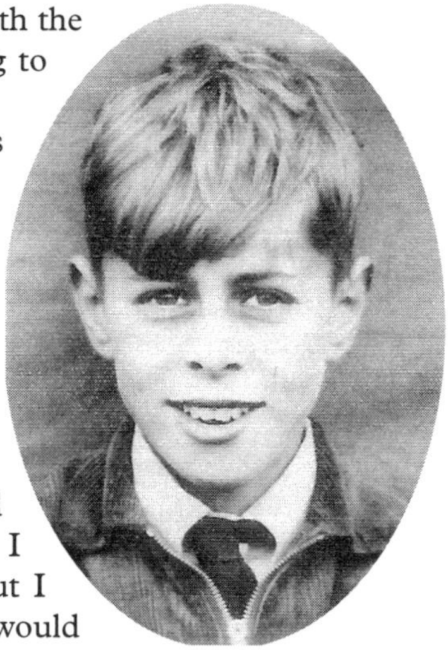

Figure 5. Mike Stringer: Agnes Road School photograph.

appreciating the wonderful illustrations on the cards I have always maintained that I learned more from reading the backs of cigarette cards that ever I learned at school! Even today, I often use the illustrations on old cigarette cards for reference in my work as an illustrator.

On Saturday mornings most of us kids looked forward to going to the cinema – either to the Ritz or my favourite, the Princess or 'Priny' where we liked to see time and time again Laurel and Hardy, the Three Stooges, Hoppalong Cassidy and other old favourites. Saturday afternoons saw me wandering around the shops in town and the markets at cleaning up time, hoping to find some item left behind amid all the cardboard boxes and rubbish.

I often enjoyed looking around the small museum situated on the top floor at the Civic Hall, looking at the stuffed birds and the other fantastic objects collected from around the world in years gone by. There were hundreds of objects displayed there, guns and swords, Zulu shields and spears, coins, butterflies and seashells, snakes preserved in jars, a huge whalebone, an Eskimo kayak, an old fire engine, as well as hundreds of stuffed birds and animals. There was no admission charge, you just climbed the stairs to the top floor and if the museum was open you went inside; if the door was locked you just wandered off to amuse yourself elsewhere.

On Sundays my sister and I sometimes went for walks, through Locke Park, past old Joe Locke and down the footpath to the yellow waters where the motorway now passes over. Or take flowers to my infant brother's grave in Barnsley Cemetery where we amused ourselves reading inscriptions on the Victorian memorials. There was little or no vandalism then and I remember those old glass domes full of faded artificial flowers placed upon graves that had been there unbroken for decades. The Whit Sunday parades came down Princess Street and I remember seeing all those huge colourful silk banners and the brass bands which were a real spectacle for a young child. I often went with my sister to visit my elderly aunt and uncle who lived at Newton Street. Auntie Jinny would usually treat us to some of her home-made jam tarts and pop. We always amused ourselves on every visit, playing with her large collection of old buttons which she kept in a large biscuit tin and looking through her collection of old postcards of music hall stars. Uncle Wilfred was deaf and dumb and was very fond of his little garden which was always full of flowers.

Sometimes we would go on the bus to visit grandma Stringer at her cottage at Skiers Spring, Hoyland. Her garden was overgrown with flowers and there was a small natural pond fed by a spring where we used to catch frog spawn and sticklebacks. She always kept a few chickens which used to sometimes come into the kitchen. The pit was close by and to one side of the cottage was an old slag heap covered in trees and, in summer, masses of dog daisies and other wild flowers. Her cottage had no modern conveniences, no gas or electricity and was lit at night with the aid of paraffin lamps. Nothing is left of her cottage today. Where it once stood is now overgrown with trees and bushes and rosebay willowherb, although the bluebell wood alongside, in Stead Lane, is still there.

The taxi cabin was soon completed and assembled at the Exchange Station Approach in 1950. At that time the number of taxis used by the public was small when compared to today. A journey by taxi was a luxury and not taken for granted. Often on weekdays my father would sit in the taxi office for two or three hours without taking a fare, despite being right next to the Bus Station and two railway stations. The other nearest taxi rank was in Peel Square. Saturdays and evenings were usually busy, so he always had two or three part-time drivers at the rank and by now he owned three cars. He always bought second-hand vehicles as he could not afford new ones and preferred Austins to any other make. In the late 1950s he bought two London-type taxis which were much better suited to the job, especially for elderly or infirm customers.

The condition of his cars had to be of a very high standard, being public service vehicles. His long-term drivers were dependable chaps and his business success very much depended on their honesty and careful driving. One particular driver who was very well spoken and dressed smartly would sometimes treat the car as though he owned it and some customers got the impression that he was the proprietor of the business. Sometimes this irritated my father but he tolerated it for a very good reason as the man always took more money than most other drivers, and if he had picked up a fare on a return journey to the taxi rank he would put it down in the office book and a note of the fare taken, something that not all the drivers bothered to do.

Although very opinionated and not always known for an even temper, my father was often very generous and when one of his drivers began working for him full-time in the 1950s he would allow him to take his taxi away on his annual holiday, complete with a full tank of petrol. He would never employ drivers who were regular drinkers or ex-army drivers, the former being in the habit of spending too long in the pubs with over-generous customers and the latter sometimes treating their taxi in a rough manner.

In common with other taxi firms, we were often busy with the wedding trade. Young couples would call into the taxi office to book their future wedding car or cars. On Saturdays my mother would put white covers on the car seats and deck the outside of the car with white ribbons etc. There must be a lot of older couples living in Barnsley who remember booking their wedding car with Station Taxis.

By 1953 (Coronation Year) our family had moved to Ardsley, where I attended Ardsley Oaks Secondary Modern School. Shortly after the Coronation, Barnsley, like a number of other towns, was preparing for the royal visit. My father had strong views on most things and disliked the royal family. He was very proud of his working class roots and a lifelong Labour voter, although he didn't have much time for those in politics or public life, whether Tory, Labour, national or local. At first he regarded the fuss and preparations in town to welcome the Queen as a waste of time and money. However, before long he also began to prepare for the big day and he put up flags and bunting around the taxi office, the Queen arriving in Barnsley at the Exchange Station. He didn't like to be outdone by anyone and if others put up flags, then he would do the same! One Christmas in the mid-1950s he put up a huge Christmas tree behind the taxi cabin, complete with lights

Figure 6. Station Taxis, Exchange Station Approach, Christmas, *c.*1955. *M Stringer*

(Figure 6). Apart from some shops, most business premises at the time weren't usually decorated much for Christmas, so his effort made a great show.

After leaving school at the age of fifteen I started work at the taxi rank, my job being to answer the phone and take bookings, as my sister had done previously when she had the same job. I liked being there as there wasn't much responsibility and it gave me ample opportunity to daydream! I had to keep the office tidy as well as make tea and run errands. Except when my old man was in a jovial mood and roaring with laughter at his own jokes, he wasn't much

Figure 7. Jack Stringer, enjoying a mug of tea, 1958. *M Stringer*

Figure 8. Mike Stringer, aged eighteen.

company during the day, spending most of the time, when not in driving, sitting reading his newspaper, smoking his Players and drinking very strong sweet tea (Figure 7).

I enjoyed the company of the railway porters down at the station and they often came into the taxi office for a chat as did some of the local 'bobbies' who appreciated the chance to have a cup of tea and a sly smoke whilst on duty. At one time there was a railway strike and my father made the taxi cabin available to the union representatives where they were able to use his telephone and make tea. After the strike was over the union presented him with an inscribed clock in appreciation of his help.

Father maintained a good relationship with the Yorkshire Traction Company at the Bus Station, although he got very annoyed at times when drivers sometimes tried to park their buses on the rank. We were allowed to use their staff canteen to buy cheap dinners.

In 1956, I was taken ill with TB and spent several months in Wath Wood Hospital. On recovering I resumed work as an office boy at the taxi rank in 1957 (Figure 8). We now had one full-time driver,

Figure 9. Station Taxi driver Phil Dawson, 1958. *M Stringer*

Figure 10. Jack Stringer (white shirt) and his drivers: Cecil, Phil Dawson, Jack Lynch and Harry Lofts, 1958. *M Stringer*

Philip Dawson (Figure 9), who as well as giving me lots of advice on life in general and girls in particular, also started to give me driving lessons. But as this took us away from the taxi office, my father stopped them. I was keen to follow the latest fashions. For a time I fell into the skiffle and rock and roll craze, my favourite singers being Elvis, Lonnie Donegan, Marty Wilde and Buddy Holly.

As well as being in attendance at the taxi rank on weekdays and Saturdays I had to be there on Saturday nights which was sometimes busy until 1am. This was the worst aspect of the taxi business as we sometimes had to put up with drunkenness amongst some of the customers. My father always carried in the car a long heavy metal torch and sometimes an iron bar, just in case of trouble, and around 1960 one of the drivers was hit over the head with a weapon by a passenger and after being hospitalised died sometime later. We were always grateful to the police for their help with troublesome customers. After making an arrest one would often say 'Never mind Jack, when we get him into the police station we'll put him straight – he will not cause any more trouble for some time!' But there were times when there was trouble at the taxi rank and we knew there was a policeman nearby 'keeping his head down', standing in the dark by Finley's shop doorway at the end of the bus station.

There were quite a lot of Hungarians living in Barnsley and they were sometimes unfairly blamed for some of the trouble in the town on Saturday nights, but I don't recall many problems involving them. There weren't many women amongst the late night customers, especially young women.

Sometimes on Saturdays my father and some of the drivers (Figure 10) would take time off to visit Oakwell to watch a football match. There was a lot of excitement and high spirits on match days but rarely any trouble. It was all much more good natured then and less aggressive than today. The football never interested me and when I could get time off from the taxi office I was more at home looking around the market or quietly browsing in WH Smiths little bookshop on Market Hill.

The annual summer holiday period was the busiest time of all for the taxis, with holidaymakers arriving off trains and coaches on Saturdays and wanting taxis to take them home. For many this was the only occasion in the year in which they would take a taxi and it would become very busy with a queue of over one hundred people at any one time, complete with all their holiday luggage. My father would invite other taxi proprietors over to help him due to the rush of custom, including Mr Sampson who normally stood with his taxi in Peel Square. At times like these my father knew there were other taxi firms, not on such friendly terms with him, who would have liked to have taken over the taxi rank at the station for themselves. He had a particular dislike for the Co-op taxi firm and he had to take particular care with fare charging. As with most taxi firms in Barnsley he did not use mileage clocks. Taxi fares were regulated by a body called the Watch Committee and the fare was set at half-a-crown (12.5p) per mile. If this fare was proved to have been exceeded a taxi firm could be put out of business. He was very resentful towards the Co-op taxis as he believed they sometimes undercharged in order to get more customers, thus competing unfairly against smaller, more vulnerable firms. The Co-op taxis could afford to run at a loss and still afford to buy brand new vehicles every few years.

The responsibility of running the taxi business was sometimes a great strain on my father, who sometimes suffered from depression as well as a bad stomach. He would often say that he wished he had

stayed a one-man, one-cab business, running his taxi from home.

In 1959 I left my job at the taxi rank and after working in Sheffield and Durham I returned to Barnsley. At the end of 1961 I left Barnsley to seek my fortune in London. The taxi business continued and during the early 1960s my father replaced the old cabin with a slightly larger more up-to-date one. He suffered a lot of ill health during the 1960s and decided to cease trading, so around 1967 he sold the business to another taxi firm. The taxi rank remained at the Exchange Station Approach until the early 1970s. The whole site has now changed, most recently through the development of the new transport interchange. My father died in 1969 and my mother, also his partner in business for all those years, passed away in 1986 (Figure 11).

Figure 11. Jack and Greta Stringer *c.*1958. *M Stringer*

5. BORN IN BARNSLEY: RAISED IN SMITHIES

by Colin Taylor

I WAS BORN in one one of the most famous coal mining towns in the world in 1924. My parents had crossed the Pennines from Littleborough in Lancashire, a mill town renowned for its woollen blankets, where, at the age of twelve, they started work. Meeting as young millworkers, their courtship lasted through the trials and parting brought on by the Great War when Father, at the age of sixteen in 1916, joined a cavalry regiment – the Fifth Inniskilling Dragoon Guards. Mother had written to Father all the time he was in the army expecting, I am sure, to take up where they had left off when he came home after the war. However, their lives were about to change quite dramatically.

Grandfather Taylor was a winder working in a colliery (Figure 1) near a small town called Wardle a few miles from Littleborough but when the mine owner decided to move to Barnsley and take over another pit, he also persuaded my Taylor grandparents to follow him, along with their twin children, my Uncle Austin and Auntie Phyllis, father's younger siblings.

All this took place while father was still in the army, so that when he had to go home it was to a town called Barnsley that I am sure he had never heard of, let alone visited, where the people, though very friendly, spoke with a strange accent that a good Lancastrian like himself could not always understand. Finding a job must have been a daunting prospect. The nearest woollen mills where he could have used his former work experience were miles away in towns like Bradford and Leeds, too far to reach on a daily basis.

He did manage to find a job, working for the town council as part of a crew that repaired and re-tarred road surfaces. Years later, whenever he spotted a crew working on a road close to where we lived, he would tell me to get ready as we were going to watch them work, as he still knew many of them, and besides the tar would help clear the

Figure 1. A miner in the cage at the small pit in Lancashire where Colin Taylor's grandfather worked. *The Author*

blockage in my nose due to my cold.

I don't know the exact date he started work as a coal miner but he did return to Lancashire to marry my mother in Rochdale on 15 July 1922, at the same church that her father and mother got married. They returned to Barnsley to live with my grandparents, a move which I later understood did not sit well with my mother, especially as my father would be out at work all day, leaving her in the hands of Leah, my grandmother, who was a bit of a nit-picker. Then, to cap it all, I came on the scene

I was born on 13 March 1924 at the Kendray Maternity Hospital, the first-born of Gilbert and Janet Taylor. At the request of my grandfather I was named Colin, his big hero being General Colin Campbell, leader of the British troops in Africa during the Boer War.

I think that it was the realisation that they had started a family and would need more living space and more money to handle things like rent, buying furniture, baby clothes etc, brought my father to the conclusion that he had to find a job that paid better. At that time and place the only place to earn more money was to go down the pit.

No doubt, like most people in the Barnsley area he had seen men with blackened faces and dirty clothes, walking along the streets on their way home from work, the brims of their flat caps pulled down at the front and the sound of their clogs echoing around the neighbourhood.

Most of the mines were located next to old villages like Carlton and Woolley that had supplied the original workers but as they grew in size the extra men needed were brought in by various forms of transport, 'paddies' being the most common. These were often converted lorries owned by individuals who most of the time used them for hauling loads of coal from wagons parked at railway sidings. At each shift change the lorries were hastily converted to passenger vehicles by placing seating benches along both sides of the truck bed and a canopy formed by a steel frame over which a tarpaulin was stretched to shelter the clients from the rain. Each paddy would carry ten to twelve miners who were picked up close to their homes and taken to a particular pit before the start of each shift and brought back home at shift end. Each rider formed a contract with a particular owner/driver, paying for one week's service in advance, usually 'tuppence a week'. As time went on paddies began to lose customers to the bus service provide by the Yorkshire Traction Company but even then many miners preferred the paddy for its companionship and its convenience.

Barnsley Council had begun building new housing estates close to the major mining areas. Each estate consisted of semi-detached houses usually arranged in ovals and avenues, each with its own garden, separated from its neighbour by a wooden fence and gates. Far removed from the old terraces, these new developments provided a very attractive and affordable home for young couples with children. Fitted with all the latest 'mod-cons', it meant that a husband could come home from the pit, covered in the usual dust and grime, and, instead of the wife having to boil kettles of water in order to fill a galvanised bath, he could walk straight into a bathroom and fill his own bath with hot water from a tap. You can feel the tremendous appeal this must have had for a young couple with a new-born child who, up to this point in their lives, had only experienced life in an old mill town on the other side of the Pennines.

Mother had agreed to cross the Pennines after marriage, and take part in raising a family and for his part, my father had committed himself to the task of providing the necessary backing in the form of a good and steady income, which, at that time and place, meant becoming a mineworker.

The prospect of a steady, relatively well-paid job, coupled with a chance to live in a modern, well-built house, sold my parents on the idea of a drastic change in lifestyle. They moved into number 14 St Helen's Avenue, Smithies, a 'council house' in the same year that I was born and in their twenty-one years of occupation I never heard them utter a word of regret.

Located on a ridge from which you could look out over the Dearne valley towards the town of Barnsley, the 'housing estate' was, at that time, surrounded by farmland and close to fascinating villages such as Monk Bretton, Carlton, Royston and Woolley. It was also close to the family source of income: Wharncliffe Woodmoor Colliery (Carlton Main). Father started working there just before we moved into number 14 and, together with Uncle Austin and several other men, who would work together on contract with the owners to produce coal at a negotiated price per ton. I always remember the rate being a constant topic of conversation whenever members of the team and the family met, or between mother and father when he came home from the union meeting in the *Wharncliffe Arms* pub.

However, as far as I was concerned, money did not seem to cause any major problems for our family or our neighbours, at least in the late twenties when I first began to be aware of such things. Everybody was well-fed and clothed according to need and occasion, whether it was for going to school, church or chapel or, to the pub on a Saturday night.

The thing that never ceased to entrance me was the transformation of these men who would come home from work in the afternoon, faces and hands blackened with coal dust to the extent that identification was difficult, their clothes wreaking of the pit; but then at the weekend the same men would be dressed in smart navy blue suits, arm in arm with elegantly dressed ladies, walking to the bus stop.

The cloth cap was replaced by the trilby, the collarless flannel shirts by white cotton shirts, complete with collars and tie. The family has a photograph of Uncle Austin taken about this time. He is dressed in a suit, black-tie and white shirt, but instead of wearing a trilby he sports a black Homburg, definitely upper crust, To cap it all, he is standing with his hands crossed on the top of a silver-capped walking stick, altogether a 'Fred Astaire about to go to the shuffle' pose. It is all the more 'Astaireish' when you realise that he is exactly the same size and shape as the famous star.

Barnsley had the largest open-air market in the country, for which it obtained its charter in the thirteenth century, and on market day people poured into town from all over the surrounding area. The stalls with their wooden frames and canvas covers were so closely packed that even on a rainy day you could walk around without getting too wet. Three fairly large open areas in the centre of town with offshoots like Market Street provided room for stalls of every variety, from fresh vegetables, to shoes, crockery, bedding and clothes. In other words, everything a woman with money in her purse could buy, and mother just loved it.

As Noel and I grew older we would get on the bus and go with Mother to the market, especially during the school summer holidays when the market stayed open until 9 pm. I really enjoyed going because not only was it a fascinating place to look at all the different produce and products but it was wonderful to hear the funny remarks of the traders, all of whom had something to say either to one and all or to one particular person. I particularly liked one of the crockery vendors. He was talking and shouting all the time, unless he was serving someone, but his skills for me lay not in his sales talk, but in his theatrical way of selling. He would pick up a couple of pieces from a set of crockery and attract people's attention by gently tapping them together and saying 'listen to that – top quality bone china, where else could you get it at this price?' While he was talking he would pick up half a dozen of the dinner plates from the same set and stack them on his right arm between his shoulder and elbow. Then he would quickly drop his arm and outstretch it in the same manner a cardsharp would use to open out a pack of cards, and the plates would slide out until stopped by his cocked fingers and lie in a cascade on his arm: 'Look at that pattern, where else but here would you see such beautiful pieces?' You don't find salesmanship like that in today's malls.

Mother was not a big spender and was always on the look-out for bargains, particular when it came to feeding two growing lads. As we grew older we would go to the market in the late evening, browse around without buying anything until fifteen or twenty minutes before 9 pm closing time, because that was when the prices came tumbling down. She would make sure we were well positioned in front of the tomato growers stall when he decided that he did not want to take what was left of his stock back to the greenhouse. 'Cum on ladies, what will you gi' me for these luvly tomatoes? I don't wanna tak em back wi me'. We would stand there until a price was agreed upon by one and all, at which time Mother would be up front buying enough to see us through till next week. We ate a lot of tomatoes in those days. Market day was Wednesday and by Saturday all traces of it ever having been there had practically disappeared, leaving wide open-spaces.

It was on Saturdays that we would visit our grandparents who lived on Cliff Terrace not far from the Oakwell Stadium. I enjoyed these visits, particularly during the football season when the town sprang back to life, but this time it was the men who filled the buses and walked around the market area looking not for bargains but for friends and, having found them, set off along Pontefract Road towards Oakwell. We would take a different route that took us up Queen's Road to the top of the ridge above the stadium which was out of sight of the field, but not out of hearing range. Every time the home team scored a goal you could hear the roar of the crowd from my grandparents' garden and beyond, so you always had a good idea of how the game was going.

Father was not a sports fan and was more anxious to set off for home before all the supporters started pouring back into the centre of town, particularly after a win when the celebrations would start. However, as we got a little older Noel and I would talk him into going back into town to see the fun because, for us, the entertainment was just beginning as the fans headed for the open market area adjoining Kendray Street. We would join them there. The attraction, for them, was the place to buy the *Green Un*, but for us, the chance to watch Gloops, the paper's salesman in action.

Gloops, a young man in his late teens or early twenties, delivered the paper to his customers, all of whom were standing around talking, by bicycle. As the sole *Green Un* salesman in that area he had to answer a call or whistle from his clients immediately, even though they were spread out over a fairly large area. He also had to be able to see where the call came from, over the heads of the crowd, and had to get over to the spot as fast as possible, carrying a large canvas bag containing his stock of papers, then stay at that spot while he delivered the paper, got paid and, if necessary, issue change. He had a modified 'sit up and beg' bicycle to suit his very demanding role. This type of bike was designed with the upper crust in mind. You could ride them in a perfectly upright position without creasing your jacket or trousers, there was no need to crouch down with your chin on the handlebars as with today's models. The handlebars were straight across, curved only at the ends where the handles and brakes were mounted. He had removed the brake handles and their attached cables and replaced them with a single steel wire cable that stretched from the rear brake to the point where the upper crossbar met the steering column. He would often 'hover' while delivering the paper or giving change, moving from call to call without putting a foot on the ground.

We would watch Gloops for as long as my father would let us but 'show over' we would head for the tram that would take us down Eldon Street as far as the junction with Old Mill Lane, the end of the line. We always got on at the Regent/Eldon Street stop for a fairly steep ride, made more thrilling for young boys as it was a double-decker tram and we always tried for the front seat of the upper deck. I got the same feeling many years later sitting at the controls of a single-engined aircraft coming in for a landing.

We would disembark and set off down Old Mill Lane for the walk home, passing the Marsden Paper Mill and the gas works, then across the Dearne bridge and on to Wakefield Road, heading for Smithies. Father always wanted to walk, no matter what the weather was like. Years later I realised how miners must have felt as it was the attraction of daylight and not the weather that encouraged walking.

I was coming up to my eighth birthday when things began to change, not just for me but for my entire family. At the beginning of the new school year I would switch – from Smithies Elementary School (Figure 2) on Wakefield Road – to Burton Road Junior School, meaning a longer walk and a different atmosphere. It was not only a larger school full of kids from other neighbourhoods but was also a demarcation line where the next three years would determine whether I would gain a place to open up a future that might lead to university education or perhaps a Trade School to learn practical skills, or even, at the age of fourteen, follow Father's footsteps and go down the mine. In other words, the final year at Burton Road was the Scholarship year when all of the students in the top class sat for an exam that only ten per cent at most would succeed and therefore transfer to either the boys' Grammar School or girls' High School in Barnsley.

Figure 2. 'Graduating' class at Smithies Infants' School, 1932. Colin Taylor is on the back row, fifth from the left. *The Author*

Mother was determined that I was going to the Grammar School. She constantly asked about my progress at school, asked me, for example, to demonstrate writing and other skills.

My brother, Noel, was born on 14 March 1929. It was the day after my fifth birthday and I remember sitting on the front step, waiting for my father to tell me when the baby had arrived. I could hear the sound of the baby crying after father had invited me in and I rushed upstairs to see a red-faced, dark-haired creature who from now on would be my younger brother. Three years later we moved up the street to 2 St Helens Avenue.

According to my father, mother had had her eye on this place ever since they moved into the area. It sat at the junction of St Helen's Avenue and Carlton Road, or Carlton Lane as it was known then, a corner plot with a large garden and, to my mother, its most important feature – the next door neighbours' side door was not looking right into your side door. It suddenly became empty and mother went into action immediately, even calling on Herbert Smith, the Mineworkers' Union leader, asking him to use his influence with the Barnsley Town Council. Father was a very active union man.

Number 2 was a great place to live. The large side garden, bordered by a privet hedge, offered a lot of privacy, especially as the house was four steps down from street level, the garden in effect hidden from the gaze of passers-by on their way to the bus stop at

the junction of the avenue and Carlton Lane. But this did not prevent
Noel and I from peering through the hedge to see who was on the
way to town. It also had a back garden where father eventually built
an aviary for budgerigars and canaries, leaving me with the job of
feeding them. The thing that intrigued me most about the place was
that my father once told us one day that although he walked every
working day down to Wharncliffe Woodmoor pit in the village of
Carlton he had to walk all the way back underground to the spot
where he was working, right under our house. The thought of my
father working down below when we were getting ready for school
had me really fascinated until one day I asked him why the concrete
step outside the side door was split in the middle and one half was
lower than other. He explained that this was because miners were
taking out the coal from the seam that ran underneath there and
Mother Nature was trying to seal the gap. He went on to say that was
why they had the occasional cave-in when sections of the roof fell,
often injuring the miners working that spot, and how they had to
keep holding the roof up with wooden beams and props. I didn't feel
so good about him being working down below us now, especially as
every day that went by the old wooden ambulance from the pit would
usually pass the end of our street, its bell ringing, on the way to
Becket Hospital, carrying yet another casualty.

Father never said much about men getting hurt down the pit,
unless it was someone we knew, like Bob Shaw, brother of Seth,
whose back was broken in a cave-in. The Shaw brothers were part of
my father's 'team', along with Uncle Austin and a couple of others.
After the operation to repair the damage Bob had to walk around in
a body cast until his back healed. He walked absolutely erect and,
unable to turn his neck in either direction. Like everyone else, our
parents just seemed to accept his predicament as part of everyday
life, not even talking about it, at least not in front of Noel and I.

We were living quite well, at least from the viewpoint of a young
boy who was more concerned about whether the rain would hold off
long enough to allow us to play football in the street than whether
new stockings were needed for Sundays but then along came the
Depression.

In 1933 Wharncliffe Woodmoor Colliery started to go on 'short-
time', so some weeks my father would work a full week but the next
only three days. On three days he could draw the dole for the shortfall.
However, if he worked one day over the three specified he did not
qualify for any unemployment pay. Father and his mates started each
week not knowing whether it was going to be a 'full-week' or not.

Usually – but not always – they were told as they checked out at the end of the third day. That is when the fun started. Nothing having been said at the end of the third day, they would turn up for work in the early hours of the next day and allowed to check in at the 'lamp oyle', receiving their lamps in exchange for their brass identification disks called 'motties'. This was the colliery's answer to punching a time clock. Then after everyone had 'checked in' and just before they went to the pithead to descend the mine they were told there was no work. This meant that they were unable to collect unemployment benefits for the balance of the week as, in theory, they had gone to work for four days in that week instead of three.

We had to cut back on such things as going to the Saturday matinee at the Empire Cinema on Eldon Street and no more Cadbury's Almond Swirls to take home for teatime desert. However, I was now old enough to join the children's section of the Barnsley Public Library, so on Saturdays we would now visit the library after a stroll around town to allow my mother to browse, buying at will was no longer on the agenda. We never realised it at the time, but this was to be a time of transition in our family's life.

Early in 1934 Uncle Austin and the Shaw brothers would persuade my father to hand in his notice at Wharncliffe Woodmoor and go with them to work at Mitchell Main Colliery, near Wombwell. From their point of view it was a good move, after all they all lived in Lundwood and could go to and from work by bus but, without a direct connection to Wombwell from our place, Father had to go by bicycle, a very common form of transport in those days. He had to leave home in the early hours of the morning on his old Wigfalls Royal single-speed bike and then ride home, mostly uphill, after a hard day's work down the pit. The coal seam was much deeper at Mitchell's and my father would talk about how hot it was underground and how barrels of water were sent down so they could slake their thirst and splash their faces in order to keep working. There was a good side to this from my point of view. Father bought a Hercules three-speed bike to make riding uphill easier and so I inherited his Wigfalls Royal and Noel got my small bike. There was another twist of fate in store for us in this year of change.

At the end of the summer holidays in 1934 I would start my final year at Burton Road Elementary, going into the 'Scholarship class' but there was a snag. Wharncliffe Woodmoor, along with most other pits in the area, closed for a week in August during the Barnsley Feast holiday, whereas Mitchell Main closed during the Wombwell feast at the beginning of September. Mother had planned on us going to visit

Figure 3. Colin, age ten (left) and Noel (5) on the Central Pier, Blackpool, summer of 1934. *The Author*

Figure 4. Gilbert and Janet Taylor, Central Pier, Blackpool, summer 1934. *The Author*

her aunt and sister in Blackpool (Figures 3-4) this holiday, now that we had a bit of money, but that meant my being out of school at the most critical time in my education. Mother decided to go and ask permission of the headmaster to take us out of school for a week. The headmaster was unconcerned at me missing lessons, saying that I would not pass the exams anyway, much to the shock of my mother.

I sat the Scholarship the following spring, followed by an interview with the school board at Barnsley Grammar School. Later, at a meeting of the entire school in the main hall, the headmaster announced that Tom Greasley, Ben Limbert, Colin Taylor and a girl whose name I can't remember, would be going on to the Grammar School and Girls' High School at the start of the next school year.

Mother's drive and desires to keep her sons out of the mine had paid off, especially when Noel followed my lead five years later. But this was only the start of the transition, from now on there would be constant change for the family, starting with the fact that I wold not be earning a wage at fourteen and our cost of living would be going up because of the expenses involved of a grammar school education. To add to the drama, my father would only work three days now and then.

At least the management at Mitchell Main did not play games with the unemployment benefits, but we still did not have enough to pay the weekly rent all on some occasions, which resulted in time in Mother, Noel and I hiding behind the couch in the front room to avoid being seen by the rent collector, a Council employee who knocked on the door and front window, yelling 'I know you are in there, I'll be back later'. Of course, the length of his round did not allow for a back-up call and my mother knew it.

Mother certainly knew how to make the money spin out. We never seemed to lack for anything at least from a young boy's perspective, especially one who now had to have new grey flannel shorts, a new jacket, ties, and a school cap. Yes, we wore shorts even in winter which led to chapped knees, a common complaint. I also needed a school bag in which to carry my books and notebooks. In those days these were made from leather, with a long shoulder strap similar to many of today's ladies' handbags.

Family bonding was a tremendous help to Noel and I. We were lucky to have parents who were against the consumption of alcohol, so they did not leave us every Saturday night to go to the pub. Instead, we all stayed at home and listened to the news from the BBC while sitting in front of the coal fire reading the books we had picked up that afternoon from the library. Father was a great believer in 'show and tell', meaning he was always eager to answer our questions in a practical way so that the information would stay with us forever. He even built his own radio with valves as big as today's light bulbs and which took up all the lower shelf of a built-in corner cupboard. He had to climb on the roof of the house to mount the aerial on the chimney. He made a square wooden frame to which he attached the aerial wire by winding it around nails set in rows down the centre of each side. The result was a spider's web that had to be hung in just the right place on the chimney to get the best reception. The radio dial was first set to a known frequency while he manoeuvred the aerial around the chimney and had Noel and I listen until the station came in loud and clear at which time we yelled 'Now!'

Building and installing your own radio became quite a hobby with some of the neighbours, as you could buy all the parts at Wigfalls in Barnsley. The hobby would later became a neighbourhood competition as to who would be the first to get 2LO, the station broadcasting in English from Luxembourg. Father won. A few years later we would listen to the same station and hear Hitler ranting and raving. I remember my father saying, 'We're goin' to have trouble with this bloke'. Building radios and other projects, however, did not stop him from carrying out his other 'show and tell' duties, namely, taking us to some place with scenic or historical features that had to be seen to be believed, and there were lots of them around the area.

Politics played an important role in our lives and local politics in particular. For the most part the miners were supporters of the Labour Party and Barnsley was of course headquarters of the Yorkshire Mineworkers' union. Father was a staunch Labour supporter, as was my mother, so Noel and I were raised in the same philosophy and we even helped out at local elections.

Elections were a fun time, especially when we attended Burton Road School. Well publicised, the approach of an election provided a chance for our pals and ourselves to express our opinion in a practical way. We would make 'conkers', not the kind that called for a Horse Chestnut to be hung from a piece of string and swung around one's head in a threatening manner, no, these were rolled up newspapers – the *Daily Herald* of course – with a string tied around the middle of the bundle and then extended out for two to three feet. Swung around the head in a manner of a cowboy winding up his lasso, it could be used to hit someone on the side of the head or in the ribs. Once fully armed we set off to find our opponents.

We knew who the local Tories were, or at least non-Labour supporters, and so we would set out to find their kids. There were one or two in the immediate neighbourhood but most lived in the 'posh' houses on the New Road or Rotherham Road as it is now called. Of course, we were expected and the 'opposition' would be waiting, armed with their versions of the 'conkers', made from copies of the *Daily Mail*. A battle would ensue, accompanied by lots of shouting and laughter, after all we would be going to school with this lot a few days later.

As children I don't think we fully appreciated the seriousness of what was now a world-wide depression. We knew our fathers were, for the most part, on 'short time' but thought that was something that only happened to coal miners and gave little attention to the side events like the rise of fascism. Father would talk about such things in the evenings, sitting in front of the fire and particularly about Sir Oswald Mosley and his British Union of Fascists who he felt would cause us a lot of trouble. Mosley had been a member of the Labour Party but in 1931 had left to start his own party, known later as the 'Blackshirts'.

I became more aware of the BUF and what it stood for at the time I started the Grammar School in 1935, because now, due to Hitler's rise to power in Germany, an anti-fascist movement was creating quite a stir in Britain and the Blackshirts were becoming unpopular and they started to lose members. This started them on a series of localised recruiting drives in the areas with large unemployment figures. I was in the middle of my second year at the Grammar School when the Blackshirts announced that they were going to visit Barnsley, with a parade and a large meeting. On the day of the big event we were warned to avoid the town centre on our way home as there might be problems.

The last class ended at 3.45 pm at which time we all aimed to be first out of the door. As Ben and I stood outside the front gate waiting for Tom Greasley so that we could walk home together, imagine our surprise when, coming through the gate, we saw our French/German teacher and our Gym teacher coming towards us dressed in slacks, open-necked shirts. Gone were the suits, ties, and black dress shoes, their normal uniform of the day. 'Where are you going sirs? 'To help the miners get rid of the Blackshirts', and get rid of them they did.

Mosley's men got a great reception, large crowd, lots of shouting, but not the hurrahs they expected but cries of 'fascists go home!', together with a lot of booing. To add injury to insult the miners rolled the Blackshirts' bus on to its side. Doing as we were told, we avoided the town centre but did see a lot of people around the fringes of the area. Of course, we got word of mouth reports later from neighbours who were in the centre of the excitement.

At about 3.15 am in the morning of Thursday, 6 August 1936 an explosion occurred at Wharncliffe Woodmoor Colliery, killing fifty-eight men, four of whom lived on our street. One of the victims, Ernest Scargill, lived directly across from us. He left a wife and three boys. Earlier, on 12 September 1935, just about the time I started the Grammar School, an explosion killed nineteen men at the North Gawber Colliery.

Accidents and explosions in the mines were always a part of the way of life in our community and somehow you never thought that your own father might one day be a name on an accident report. I was so wrapped up in the thought that I would be starting at the Grammar School that I never paid much attention to the North Gawber disaster but the situation at Carlton changed all that. Father would return there soon after the explosion and help in the clean up and rebuilding, but not for long.

Father would leave the mine for good and from that point on our lives would change. Of all things, he became the head malster at the Barnsley Brewery and was a good supervisor. In 1938, as the crisis in Europe became more serious, he volunteered as a part-time Air Raid Warden and at the start of the war changed to being an officer in the National Fire Service and fought fires in Hull, Liverpool and other places (Figure 5). I would

Figure 5. Gilbert Taylor (in National Fire Service uniform), Patrol Leader, outside a converted warehouse which served as the local station. To his left is son, Colin (in Air Cadet uniform), aged fifteen and youngest son, Noel, aged nine. The car was used to to tow the mobile fire pump. *The Author*

Figure 6. Colin Taylor on leave from Africa at the end of the war. This photograph was taken just before he went to Leeming in North Yorkshire where he met Eileen, his future wife. *The Author*

eventually join the RAF (Figure 6) and become a pilot and while awaiting demobilisation at the end of the war would meet a WAAF who worked in the Met Office at RAF Leeming in North Yorkshire who would become my wife.

After all the excitement and travel we had experienced in the Air Force it was difficult for us to settle down. In December 1953 I set off to take up a job in Hamilton, Ontario. Eileen, my wife, and our two children, came to Hamilton in March of '54, once I had saved enough money for their fares on the ship. Our daughter was going on four and our son had his first birthday on the ship. After three years in Canada we thought we would try the United States and so in the summer of 1957 moved to Buffalo, New York. Two years in Buffalo convinced us that there must be a better place to raise kids, so in 1959 we moved to San Francisco, California. The sixties were a turbulent time in and around San Francisco and, having visited Oregon on business, we (just Eileen and myself as our son and daughter were at university) moved to Portland in September 1970. We have now lived in Lake Oswego, Oregon longer than we have lived in England, so when we meet people for the first time they ask me 'How come you still have an English accent?' In true Barnsley fashion I tell them 'I practice in front of the mirror every night'. Seriously, though, I'm proud to have been born and brought up in Smithies, near Barnsley, places I will never forget.

6. POSTCARDS FROM BARNSLEY

by Norman Ellis

I WAS IN BARNSLEY BUS STATION, clutching my OAP pass in readiness for my return journey to Wakefield, when a large assortment of bags and packages suddenly appeared beside me. Somewhere in the middle of them, panting slightly, was a small lady. I made the obvious remark that she looked 'loadened'. To which the lady replied that she was only going home because she had left a plumber doing jobs in her house and wished to get back before he left. She added, 'Have just seen a nice pair of trousers, but didn't have time to try them on, so I'll have to come again.' She used the next few minutes to extol the virtues of shopping in Barnsley.

To be honest, I prefer Barnsley as it used to be (Figures 1 & 2). It has lost much of its character. On the plus side, it now has the

Figure 1. Market day on Cheapside. To the left is Edward Bailey's drapery store. Uncle Reg posted the card from Barnsley to his neice, May, in London on 22 November 1924. 'Tell daddy I have just seen a football fight. Some game. I will send you some cigarette cards. Hope you are a good little girl. If so, will give you something nice for Xmas. Will see you then'. *C & A G Lewis of Nottingham postcard no. 467.*

Figure 2. Queen Street, looking towards Peel Square. Perhaps the parson, having purchased a packet of tea at the Maypole Dairy shop, is on his way to Jackson's for a new hat. The C & A G Lewis 'Robin Hood Brand' card no. 469, was posted from Barnsley to Norwich in April 1926.

Figure 3. Typical of the work of Gothard is this montage of the Yorkshire Agricultural Show, held on Dodworth Road, Barnsley in 1907. Portraits of Viscount Halifax, the President, plus the mayor and deputy mayor, are accompanied by three views of the showground, the upper and lower ones being juxtapositions of separate photographs (the joints are just visible). The card was posted from Barnsley to Morecambe on 16 August 1907, six days after the event closed.

excellent all-weather Alhambra and Metropolitan shopping centres. A recently published brochure describes the market as 'bigger, brighter and busier than ever.' The shopping centre, with its major high street retailers, is described as a 'shopping paradise.' Where, though, is the town that I knew on my way to run amok in Locke Park? Or, to move back even further, the Barnsley I see on my collection of old postcards. The town had some outstanding photographers, whose work, much of it consisting of sharp and superbly animated street scenes, appeared on postcards. The excellence of their work was due, in part, to the background tapestry of interesting buildings.

The work of Barnsley-based Warner Gothard (Figure 3) and his sons is familiar to most postcard collectors. Their commemorative montages include some Barnsley events. The firm also produced ordinary photographic cards of the Barnsley area. For more comprehensive representation of Edwardian and post-Edwardian Barnsley, we need to turn to various other Barnsley photographers and a few national postcard producers. Two national firms – Valentine of Dundee and C & A G Lewis of Nottingham – produced some excellent photo images of the town (Figures 1 & 4). Amongst the local photographers, Thomas Lamb of 80 Racecommon Road and later of 49 Dodworth Road, stands way ahead for extent of postcard output. Examination of his handiwork reveals that it is pin-

Figure 4. Eldon Street, with the Harvey Insitute (later the Public Hall), on the left, c.1905. The trough, tramlines and railway bridge are a reminder of three forms of transport in the town - horse, electric and steam. The John J Mallison shop on the right sold rope, twine and mats. *A Valentine of Dundee card (no. 80452).*

Figure 5. Queen Street in the early 1930s. A forerunner to post-war changes was the widening of the street in 1930. The north side, including the Maypole, was swept away and new property erected, shown on the right. The rebuilt *Royal Oak Hotel* and new Woolworths can be seen. The Yorkshire Traction Leyland Titan bus also helps to date the Lamb photograph.

Figure 6. Peel Square, with the *Barnsley Chronicle* building, now *The Chambers*, formerly *Tommy Wallocks* pub, in the centre. Horse-drawn transport predominates, including two milk floats, but a lone car infiltrates. This card is so sharp that, aided by a glass, most of the shop window signs can be read. High praise for Thomas Lamb, the photographer. The card was posted from Barnsley to Hemel Hempstead in 1910.

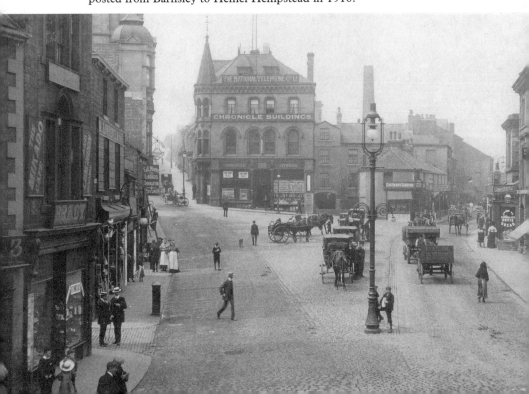

sharp, correctly exposed, and crammed with interest (Figure 6).

Aspects of life in the industrial-based town of Barnsley were favourably covered by a large number of excellent postcards. Many of them are quite scarce and soon snapped up. For this article I have tried to use the less-familiar or previously unpublished views.

Barnsley owes some of its growth to the linen industry. By the beginning of the last century, this had drastically declined and had been overtaken by coal mining. The town became a recognised coal capital. The mineworkers' offices on Huddersfield Road, featured on many postcards, were opened in 1874. The Mining and Technical College was opened in October 1932. Built next to it, the Town Hall was opened in December 1933. Barnsley became a popular venue for miners' demonstrations. The South Yorkshire Miners' Association was established in 1858 and Barnsley was chosen as the location of its first demonstration in 1863. Between 1897 and 1911, six of the fifteen demonstrations were held there. (The South Yorkshire and West Yorkshire Miners' Association had amalgamated in 1881).

The erection of artisan housing had proceeded apace after 1850, much of it in the areas surrounding Town End, where linen mills and some engineering works had been located. With two railway stations (three if we include Summer Lane), the Barnsley Canal and eventually a tramway system, the town seemed destined to prosper (Figures 7, 8 & 11).

Figure 7. Opening of Town End Recreation Ground, 29 June 1905. In the left background are the Summer Lane Saw Mills of W G & L England. The small park and nearby Olympia Skating Rink were havens of recreation in an otherwise industrial area of Barnsley.

Figure 8. Tramcar no.10 of the Barnsley & District Traction Company passes the Mason drinking fountain on Sheffield Road. The stylish houses were three-quarters of a mile from the town centre. Romance was in the air when Sydney posted the Thomas Lamb card (in an envelope) from Barnsley to his beloved on 30 November 1912. The message reads: 'My own loving sweetheart, hope you are having better weather in Norwich than we are just now. It is bitterly cold, and very dangerous walking with the ice and snow. Longing for Sunday morning when I shall hear from you again. It seems a long time from Tuesday. Hope you get this Sunday morning. With all my heart's love, ever yours, Sydney'.

As a shopping and trading centre for the surrounding colliery villages it was second to none (Figures 9, 10 & 12). Many of the Victorian buildings became soot-blackened – and more aesthetically pleasing to some eyes.

Butterfield's Drapery Store was established at 1 Church Street in 1901. It subsequently took in numbers 3 and 5 and became Butterfields and Massies. Butterfields were renowned for their extensive advertising. From a bonnet to a bedstead, a dress skirt to a

Figure 9. *Trafalgar Hotel*, New Street. Originating in 1841, the last pints were pulled here in 1961. The card was posted from Barnsley to a Mr Simpson, caretaker of Royston cemetery, on 13 August 1908, with the request, 'Please attend to our son's grave at your earliest if it is convenient. I should like it sown with grass seed, and will pay for when done'.

Figure 10. John F Barraclough used these premises at West Terrace, Westgate as a bottling depot until *c.*1930, when they were taken over by William Dugdale, who continued the business. The postcard was sent from Barnsley to Blackpool in 1923.

Figure 11. An uncaptioned, uncredited but very detailed image (possibly by Lamb) of Wyman's bookstall at Barnsley Court House Station. The former Court House actually housed the station's ticket office. Visible in addition to books are placards for now-dufunct magazines, a display stand of postcards and a clock by Potts of Leeds. The suspended lamp carries the word 'Barnsley'. The station was opened in 1870 and closed to passengers in 1960.

Figure 12. Maypole Dairy shop, Queen Street. The display consists entirely of Maypole brand butter, margarine and tea. This card, by Lamb of Barnsley, was sent by Ethel from Taylor Hill to a friend in Moldgreen, Huddersfield, in the 1920s with a tale of woe: 'Sorry to disappoint you, but I have been bad all week with a swollen knee. It is not better yet. I can't bear to walk on it much. So I shall have to rest it and try to get it better'.

tea d'oyley, a pram cover to a pelisse – Butterfields supplied it. Fur coats were stocked in great variety, including sable, fox, wallaby and squirrel – to name just a few.

The Barnsley British Co-operative Society was founded in 1862. It had several shops in the town and many others in outlying villages. By 1902 the membership had reached 20,781. One of the attractions was the dividend or 'divi' which then stood at just over half-a-crown (12.5p) in the pound. This was a useful bonus for working-class people. The town also gave its name to the Barnsley Brewery Company on Pontefract Road. Their Brown Stout and Light Ale cost 2s 6d (12.5p) per dozen bottles in 1903. The Britannia Brewery Company, of Sheffield Road, advertised their 'Very Strong' at 1s 6d (7.5p) per gallon in 6, 9, 12 and 18 gallon casks.

Barnsley's main park was of course named after Joseph Locke, the great railway engineer. Born in Attercliffe, Sheffield, in 1805, he soon moved to Barnsley with his parents. After attending the local

Figure 13. The Obelisk at the top of Church Street. It was erected in 1819 as a guidepost for travellers at a busy crossroads. It became a victim of flyposting, was later regarded as an obstruction, but not knocked down until 24/25 September 1931. An unidentified photographer recorded the action. Stretching into the distance is Huddersfield Road, whilst the miners' offices and memorial are visible on the left.

Figure 14. An all-male contingent awaits departure of a charabanc trip from the *Cross Keys Hotel* on May Day Green. The vehicle, built on a Dennis chassis, was on hire from George Booker, Peel Street, the town's best-known cab and charabanc proprietor.

grammar school, he trained as a colliery manager in Durham. Returning to Barnsley, he worked in the offices of his father's colliery, and was sometimes called upon to deliver coal. Joseph Locke's father was a friend of George Stephenson, the railway engineer. Young Locke entered Stephenson's works at Newcastle and by his genius became engineer-in-chief during the construction of the Liverpool to Manchester Railway. He was elected as President of the Institute of Civil Engineers and in 1847 became MP for Honiton in Devon. Locke died in 1860. In his memory, Locke's widow gave £1,830 for sixteen acres of land known as High Style Fields. After enclosing and

Figure 15. Montage to celebrate the appearance of Barnsley FC in the quarter final of the FA Cup in 1907. They were defeated 0-1 by Woolwich Arsenal. The card, in similar vein to a Gothard, was produced by George Washington Irving, photographer and picture-frame maker of Eldon Street and Sheffield Road. It was posted from Worsbrough Bridge to Chesterfield on 11 March 1907.

laying out the land, she presented it to the town. In 1877, the sister of Mrs Locke added another twenty acres to the park.

Bits of older Barnsley, which I see in my old postcards, remain, but the town has changed radically and is still in a state of flux. I am told that the younger generation like it, so who am I to argue? On a recent visit, I was held up for five minutes at the town's level-crossing whilst two trains passed through. In its way, that was a fragment of the past. If only they had been steam trains!

The images used in this article are from my postcard collection. Many of them have been thankfully expertly reproduced by Chris Sharp of *Old Barnsley*, at Unit 14 in the Upper Market Hall, making them more widely available.

Acknowledgement

The above is an adaptation of an article by Norman Ellis which appeared in the December 2001 issue of *Picture Postcard Monthly*. This well-illustrated magazine is published by Reflections of a Bygone Age, 15 Debdale Lane, Keyworth, Nottingham, NG12 5HT (Telephone: 0115 937 4079).

7. EDMUNDS AND SWAITHE MAIN COLLIERIES

by John Goodchild, M Univ

THE EDMUNDS AND SWAITHE MAIN collieries developed in
*c.*1855 and 1860 respectively, in the already industrialised valley of
the River Dove at Worsbrough, to the south of Barnsley. The year
1804 had witnessed the opening of the final and uppermost section
of the Dearne and Dove Canal Company's main line through to
Barnsley from Swinton on the River Don, and its connection with
the Barnsley Canal which ran from near Silkstone via Barnsley to
Wakefield on the navigable Calder, and 1804 also saw the opening of
the Dearne & Dove's branch canal along the Dove valley for over two
miles to Worsbrough Bridge, alongside the Wakefield & Sheffield
turnpike road. As early as 1802 an advertisement in the *Leeds
Intelligencer* had offered to let a colliery at Swaithe, with a shaft sunk
near the canal branch then under construction, but there was to be
little development industrially in that valley and neighbourhood until
the 1820s and 1830s.

The only major colliery in the valley immediately subsequent to
the opening of the canal was that owned by Francis Edmunds of
Worsbrough Hall who died in 1825, aged eighty-nine. Soon
afterwards, Edmunds's erstwhile agent, Andrew Faulds, already a
partner in the Worsbrough Furnace and a partner in an iron foundry
at Barnsley, took partners in the coal business as Field, Coopers &
Faulds. By 1840 a flint glass works, lime kilns, twenty-one coke
ovens, boat yards, a paper mill and a boiler works had all been
established at Worsbrough. William White's trade directory of 1838
referred to the Dale as 'presenting a scene of bustle not often
excelled in market towns.'

Although the North Midland Railway had opened in 1840 it was
not possible to use it for the carriage of coal to London. By the 1830s
increasing but small amounts of coal were being taken by sea to
London but it was not until the mid-1840s that the promotion,
Parliamentary authorisation and then the beginning of the
construction of other railways connecting the coalfield with London
first offered to capitalists the real prospect of major new south of
England markets, and plans were then prepared for developing new
collieries. The Darley Main Colliery opened 1834-38, soon to be

followed by Bell Ing, the direct forerunner of Edmunds and Swaithe, which began to produce coal about the middle of 1848 and was located not only conveniently close to the canal basin at Worsbrough Bridge, but also close to the line of a projected London-connecting railway. In 1847 an Act was obtained to build the South Yorkshire, Doncaster & Goole Railway, with a branch to Worsbrough opened within three years. The 'South Yorkshire' connected with the Great Northern Railway, whose line to London via the Boston loop was opened in 1850, and direct from 1852.

The new Bell Ing Colliery was promoted by Shepherd & Co, who began negotiations for a coal lease from the Elmhirst family in 1845. William Shepherd was a Barnsley lawyer and had been a partner with Jonas Clark (d.1822), the Barnsley lawyer and Silkstone coalmaster. In Darley Main Colliery one of the partners was another Barnsley lawyer, now turned linen manufacturer and colliery owner, Henry Jackson.

Shepherd & Co's Bell Ing Colliery eventually had three working shafts and an air shaft, with a tramway crossing the turnpike, leading down to the canal basin. The partners found the commercial going hard and by the middle of 1851 coal production had ceased. Bell Ing remained unworked until the following May when the lease was taken over by Joseph Mitchell, consisting of some thirty acres of Barnsley Bed coal for a term of thirty years. Joseph Mitchell had been apprenticed to a boilermaker at the Milton Ironworks near Elsecar, become a journeyman at Barnsley and elsewhere before taking a small foundry at Worsbrough between 1838-40. His boiler works grew so that by 1848 he was described as an ironfounder and boilermaker, by 1857 as an engineer and ironfounder, and later as a manufacturer of railway wagons.

Mitchell may have been short of capital in his growing businesses, or he may simply have decided to amalgamate with potential rivals, as he became a partner with John Tyas and Charles Bartholomew, the railway and canal engineer, who, in 1854 had taken another thirty years' lease of the Barnsley Bed coal from the Martin family, the new owners of the Worsbrough Hall estate. Each partner was assumed to have already advanced £1,200, and was expected to add a further £1,000. The leases extended to 350 acres (90 belonging to Mitchell) and on the amalgamated royalty a new pit was to be sunk with the name Edmunds Main.

The new partners were interesting men, and as Bartholomew and Tyas were to remain involved with the new colliery for effectively its whole working life, and as that association was in each case a real and regular one, something of their life stories may be told. Charles Bartholomew was born at Birstal in 1806 and by 1836 he was engineer to the opulent and powerful Dun Navigation, as were to be his brother and nephew successively for the even more powerful Aire and Calder Navigation. By 1837 Bartholomew was living in Rotherham; from 1840 he was manager and engineer to the Don Navigation, and from 1845 local engineer to the South Yorkshire Coal Railway, and subsequently to the South Yorkshire, Doncaster & Goole Railway, earning a substantial £1,000 a year salary. He was to retain his Dun offices and salary and divide his time between the two concerns. He was said to 'personify the South Yorkshire'. In his railway work he met Dr Robert Dymond, chairman of the South Yorkshire Railway at various periods. He also met Samuel Roberts junior, a director of that company, and Robert Baxter, its Doncaster lawyer, and it was with these partners that Bartholomew was to join in sinking Wombwell Main and Cortonwood collieries. Bartholomew ultimately joined the board of the SYR, and in the mid-1870s he moved to live at Castle Hill House at Ealing, although he retained his colliery interests and was for many years the managing director at Wombwell Main, but constantly consulted as to Edmunds and Swaithe. He was deeply interested in matters ecclesiastical and in 1854 published *The Life and Doctrine of Jesus Christ*. Outside the world of canals and railways, Bartholomew was in 1857 co-patentee of machinery for rolling railway tyres, and in the 1860s he was a partner in the Rotherham Flax Mill Company. He died in 1895, aged eighty-eight.

The other new partner in the Edmunds & Swaithe Main company was John Tyas (1817-95), a Barnsley lawyer. Tyas was the first Clerk to the Barnsley Poor Law Guardians, and served as Superintendent Registrar, was active in local politics as a Tory and was a member of the Barnsley Local Board and its successor, the Corporation, becoming successively councillor, alderman and mayor (in 1870 and again in 1883). A High Churchman, he was warden of St Mary's and influential in the establishment of the town's Mechanics' Institute and Public Hall. Like Mitchell, he was a prominent Freemason.

The new partnership of 1854 sank their new Edmunds Main colliery to the Barnsley Bed at about 105 yards and opened coal production there in *c.*1855. The shafts lay to the south of both canal and railway, in open fields between them and the Worsbrough Dale Gunpowder Mills. From 1857 negotiations for additional areas of coal lower down the valley were in progress, and there was some opposition from one important land and coal owner owing to the increasingly influential Bartholomew being a partner, but the new leases were signed in 1859, with significant legal costs of £414, and so Swaithe Main was opened in 1860. Here, the Barnsley Bed was reached at some 230 yards, faults and dipping strata accounting for the increased depth compared with Edmunds. Swaithe lay conveniently close to the railway and canal, and both means of transport were used from this colliery too.

The coal sent from Edmunds via the Great Northern Railway increased rapidly in the late 1850s, reaching 14,674 tons in 1858, dropped dramatically (only 327 tons) in 1863 (after the explosion) and then rose again to 5,364 tons in 1865.

In 1867 a block of coal weighing seven tons and occupying two men for seven days in its hewing, was sent to the Paris Exhibition from Edmunds Main. When got, it weighed nearly eight tons, but was too large to be transported along the pit's underground roadways.

The workings of Edmunds Main and Swaithe Main were connected underground in November 1863. Bell Ing Colliery was formally abandoned by the firm, who seem to have sub-let its coal to the Darley Main Company and later to Cooper and Co (late Field, Cooper & Faulds), who retained the sub-lease until 1868.

In December 1862, during the winter months, there occurred the first of the large disasters connected with these collieries and which were to bring them both considerable public prominence. Edmunds Main was then described as

not only one of the most extensive, but has always been considered one of the safest, best ventilated, and best managed in South Yorkshire

with Mitchell as managing partner and George Lawton as underground manager. The workings then extended from east to west for almost one mile, and near the western extremity, underground roadways were being driven to connect up with Swaithe Main. It was in these headings that a fire broke out, when 200 men and boys were in the pit and 51 were killed. Two explosions took place and several men, including the underground manager, were killed by the second blast, and it was ultimately decided to flood the mine in order to extinguish the fire (Figures 1 & 2). The workings remained flooded until June 1863, after which they were found 'completely free of gas' and naked lights were used in them.

A coroner's inquest was opened on the day after the explosions, before Thomas Taylor, the Wakefield lawyer, coroner and historian, with Charles Morton, the regional Mines Inspector, William Stewart, the Wakefield lawyer (and himself a partner in Lundhill Colliery)

Figure 1. How the explosion was shown in *The Illustrated London News*. *Brian Elliott*

Figure 2. A trench was cut from the Dearne & Dove Canal in an attempt to flood the mine (from *The Illustrated London News*). *Brian Elliott*

appearing for the colliery owners, and William Henry Gill, another
Wakefield solicitor, appearing for the relatives of the deceased. The
inquest was adjourned to various subsequent dates, the jury bringing
in a verdict of 'accidental death' but adding a rider deprecating the
use of blasting by gunpowder. One juryman handed to the coroner a
protest which explicitly condemned the use of powder in an
obviously gas-filled atmosphere, and claiming that this aspect of the
running of the pit

> *without the supervision of a competent coal viewer, was a*
> *criminal neglect of reasonable care and caution on the part*
> *of the managing partner, Mr. Joseph Mitchell.*

The list of deaths showed that the majority of workmen lived close to
the pit, almost entirely in Worsbrough Dale and Worsbrough
Common. The widows, with the backing of the Miners' Association,
began proceedings against the colliery owners to obtain
compensation under the provisions of the *Lord Campbell's Act*. The
cases were tried at York Assizes in March 1864, but the owners, while
denying all legal liability, proposed to pay the widows £1,550, on
their agreeing to withdraw all thirty-four actions and pay their own
costs. This was the first time in England that compensation for loss
of life had been obtained under the Act. A subscription list had
already been opened for the relief of the widows and children to be
in addition to relief granted by the Guardians, and the company
headed the list with £200; among many other donations, a gift of
£200 was received from Queen Victoria.

The twin collieries were described in October 1871, in the
Barnsley Chronicle, as being about a mile apart. At Edmunds Main
the headgear was 56ft high and a pulley 9ft in diameter worked single
decked cages from a depth of about 105 yards, in two drawing shafts
of 10ft and 9ft diameter, using a 30hp winding engine with a
pumping engine in the same house. At the shaft bottom a pair of
hauling engine twin stroke cylinders pulled loads of 16.5 cwt corves
along inclines of a thousand yards. A Bailey of Wakefield telegraph
system was in use underground, and a mining system with bords and
banks, with wide pillars was in operation. The pit was about to
introduce John Mitchell's twin-decked cages.

At Swaithe Main, another 56ft high pitchpine headgear carried
17ft pulleys, and a pair of 60hp winding engines wound a 17ft drum.
Here, the drawing and upcast shafts were of the more modern
dimensions – each 13ft, with the latter shaft increasing to 15ft at the
bottom, near which was the ventilating furnace, which had a wrought

Figure 3. Edmunds Main Colliery in 1859, an illustration from *The Illustrated London News*. *John Goodchild Collection*

iron chimney carried up the shaft of about 230 yards. The coal here was about 8ft 6 inches thick. Surface hauling engines of 30hp were connected by steel ropes to their load on the underground powered incline, the coal to the dip being worked thus, and that to the rise by self-acting inclines. The lessees were the Bishop of Llandaff and J M Gaskell of Wakefield. In full work, the colliery could pull some 7,800 tons a week, much of it sent to the London and Southern coal markets.

The situation of Edmunds Main is well illustrated in an engraving published in 1859 (Figure 3). Its coal lease expired in 1888 and pillars only had been then worked in the coal for at least a year. When the partners did decide to work deeper seems, the shafts were considered too narrow, at 9ft and 10ft, while at Swaithe the screens and the way to the canal both needed repair, and the location of the railway sidings was regarded as inconvenient. The Blacker Main site was considered as more suitable for any new sinkings, with its one 13ft furnace shaft.

An explosion of firedamp, where powder was used in a fiery mine, occurred at Swaithe Main almost thirteen years after that at

Figures 4-5. The Swaithe Main explosion of 1875: above and below ground. From *The Illustrated London News*. *John Goodchild Collection*

Edmunds, in December 1879 (Figures 4 & 5). A very high total of 143 men and boys were killed, making this one of the worst of British colliery disasters. The situation was described in the London press; a list of those killed detailed names, work done, addresses and family details; money was raised by public appeal and the sale of special commemorative pottery plates, and the surplus monies were use to finance the foundation of the West Riding Miners' Permanent Relief Fund.

Three years after the Edmunds Main disaster, a memorial was opened, and sited near to the door of St Thomas' Church in Worsbrough Dale (Figure 6). Alderman Tyas had given £50 towards its cost.

The Swaithe Main disaster was followed by a dispute between the partners as to the amount which should be given to the relief fund which was again got up. Bartholomew was willing to give £1,000 from the firm, and Tyas £3,000. In the event, the firm gave £1,000 and Tyas another £1,000 personally, while a deputation to London resulted in £2,500 from the Mansion House Fund and smaller subscriptions from colliery firms, coal owners, private persons, societies and so forth. By July 1876 it was estimated that the total would be £10,000. Meanwhile there was criticism via the Mines Inspector of bad lamp maintenance, poor air distribution, the use of powder for blasting and the non-ventilation of goafs (waste areas), although there was no proof as to how the explosion occurred. As the disaster fund was being organised it was reported that 'a good deal

Figure 6. The memorial to the Swaithe Main disaster, St Thomas' churchyard, Worsbrough Dale. *Brian Elliott*

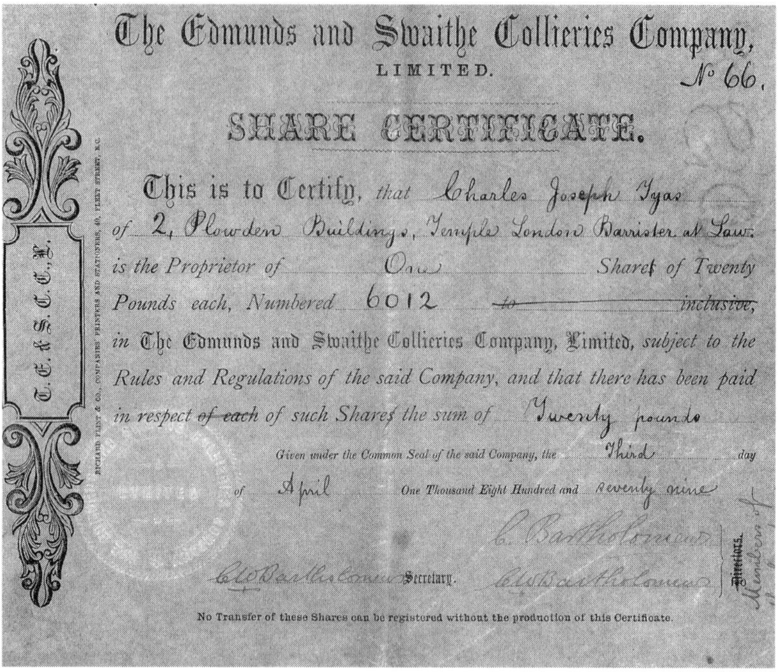
The Edmunds and Swaithe Collieries Company,
LIMITED. No 66.
SHARE CERTIFICATE.
This is to Certify, that Charles Joseph Tyas
of 2, Plowden Buildings, Temple London Barrister at Law.
is the Proprietor of One Share of Twenty
Pounds each, Numbered 6012 ~~to inclusive,~~
in The Edmunds and Swaithe Collieries Company, Limited, subject to the Rules and Regulations of the said Company, and that there has been paid in respect of ~~each~~ of such Share the sum of Twenty pounds
Given under the Common Seal of the said Company, the Third day of April One Thousand Eight Hundred and seventy nine
C. Bartholomew — Directors. Members of
C W Bartholomew Secretary. C W Bartholomew
No Transfer of these Shares can be registered without the production of this Certificate.
C. E. & S. C. L.
RICHARD FLINT & CO. COMPANIES PRINTERS AND STATIONERS, 40, FLEET STREET, E.C.

Figure 7. An Edmunds & Swaithe Collieries Co., Ltd., share certificate of 1879. *John Goodchild Collection*

of distress is being witnessed among the bereaved.'

In September 1875, Mitchell had reached the Barnsley Bed at his new colliery, Mitchell Main, in coal leased near Aldham Junction, below Swaithe Main; his partners were Mr Worms, the great Paris coal merchant, and H Josse of Grimsby. But Mitchell was claimed at the time to have been much affected by the Swaithe disaster of the end of that year; he was also a busy man as a Union Guardian, chairman of the Worsbrough Local Board, on the School Board and an active Freemason, until his death, in January 1876. He was buried in St Thomas's churchyard and a Memorial Hall subsequently built at Worsbrough Dale. Mitchell was succeeded by his wife and their two sons, and it was from that, for £18,232, Tyas and Bartholomew bought Mitchell's one-third share in Edmunds and Swaithe, in April 1878.

In February 1879 the partners turned the concern into a limited liability company, with the substantial capital of £125,000, but without participation by persons outside the two families concerned (Figure 7). The subscribers were:

Charles Bartholomew C E (Castle Field House, Ealing)
Sarah Hammond Bartholomew, spinster
Rev Charles Fred Cumber West, parson (Charlbury, Oxfordshire)
Chas Wm Bartholomew, CE, (Blakesley Hall, Northumberland)
John Tyas, solicitor (Upperwood Hall, Darfield)
Chas John Tyas, barrister (Temple, London)
Arthur Rock Tyas, gent (Upperwood Hall)
Mary Agnes Tyas, spinster (Upperwood Hall)

John Mammatt of Leeds was consulting engineer and Bartholomew, from distant Ealing, kept a careful eye on the colliery concerns. Traffic was by both rail and canal carriage to Hull, Goole, Grimsby, Doncaster and King's Cross. The firm rented its own sidings at Doncaster and London, and used the services of South Yorkshire Steam Coal Owners' Association offices in Hull and London. The railway serving the valley's collieries was doubled in 1877 and was extended in 1880 to meet the direct line to Penistone and Manchester, opening out a direct route to Lancashire and North Western coal markets. The use of Worsbrough canal branch for coal carriage was also continued by Swaithe Main. The major trouble with maintaining the canal was the subsidence caused by the working of coal below it, for while coal for support could be bought by the canal's owners, the canal's income was insufficient to warrant the considerable cost involved. In January 1867 the Edmunds partnership had given notice to the canal owners that the coal under the canal branch was to be worked, but the railway had not exercised its powers to purchase: the coal was worked and the consequent subsidence, faced in June 1884, caused part of the canal to collapse, flooding the railway and costing almost £19,000 to make good. The colliery partners then decided to make a contribution of £500 towards repairs and to leave supporting pillars; the canal was closed for six months. Another bank slip occurred in 1886, by which time only Swaithe Main used the canal to any extent and the whole of the Dearne and Dove provided little income for its railway owners. In 1889, the canal was still in use, but was regarded by both its owners and nearby colliery owners, as of little significance for the carriage of coal, but it was until 1934 that the last boat passed through the entire main line of the canal. Although Swaithe Main closed as a working colliery in 1896, the Worsbrough branch canal survived in navigable condition until the end of 1905. In November of that year the bank of the branch burst at Lewden and abandonment came in 1906. Nowadays, some parts of the branch canal appear to be on an actual gradient, so marked has been the subsidence from which it has suffered.

It is not clear if railway or canal-borne coal is alluded to when, in 1879, the colliery writes that 'We are sending 555 tons to Hull this week. We are receiving 6/- per ton for the above order at the pit', while the depression of the 1870s is mirrored in the comment that 'The Coal Owners [of South Yorkshire] have been working without profit for years past, some at a great loss.'

The annual statements of the new limited liability colliery company from 1879 show the concern enjoying a relatively healthy financial situation in a period of depression regionally and nationally (figure rounded to the nearest £100):

Year	Coal Sales (£)	Wages Paid (£)	Profit (£)
1879	53,800	40,400	?
1880	72,000	48,300	3,230
1881	73,000	48,400	4,343
1882	74,500	47,200	7,267
1883	83,800	50,400	14,570
1884	78,700	50,500	7,571
1885	76,700	51,400	9,015
1886	70,800	51,200	709

The percentage of sales income paid as wages varied between 75% (1879), 60% (1882) and 72% (1886). The profits, as representing an averaged return over the period on the £108,000 of issued capital, were 6.2% a year – a substantial return in this period of depression. No detailed returns survive between 1887-93 and when the series begins again the situation was very different. The coal sales figures of 1894, at £44,291 and the wages total of £28,720 show a considerable diminution in coal output, and in the first half years of the ensuing 1895 and 1896 show a rapidly deteriorating position:

Year	Coal Sales (£)	Coke Sales (£)	Coal and Coke Sales (£)	Wages (£)
1.6.1895	44,300	–		28,700
1.6.1896	15,500	–		12,200
1897	–		5,600	1,734
1898		5,717		3,960

This chart conceals an even more interesting picture, revealed by the statement for the first half of 1897, when coke production was 685 tons in probably the first period of coke's large-scale production, and when only seventeen tons of coal were sold, wages were about £90. Coal production had ceased and the batteries of coke ovens became the company's sole raison d'etre. The limited potential of the colliery as a coal producer had been recognised when the new limited company was being formed: in June 1878, of the leased Barnsley Bed area of some 795 acres, some 40% only remained to get.

The new Edmunds & Swaithe company of 1879 was essentially a reconstitution of the old partnership, the only additional members of the new company being members of their families and given small numbers of shares. The expended capital of the concern was, to 31 March 1885, £138,174 plus £4,925 in the farm and in its stock. The company seems never to have been successful, compared with its near neighbours, Wombwell or Lundhill. For a time, however, it was among the largest employers of labour in the South Yorkshire Coalfield. In February 1864 there were 354 employees on strike and in July 1874, 700. By 1879 there were 1,000 employees. Certainly in 1874, Edmunds & Swaithe, with 700 employees, employed similar numbers to Wombwell Main and more than Lundhill's 550, Darley Main's 400 or Strafford Main's 560, but its numbers were less than the 950 at Wharncliffe Silkstone, Thorncliffe's 1,050 and the (Old & New) Oaks' 1,200.

Although little survives in relation to the disposal of coal from the collieries prior to the 1880s, there is then a plethora of references which seem to propose that the two largest markets – that eastwards to the seaboard at Goole, Hull and Grimsby, that southwards to London – were served through local coalmasters' consortia of which Edmunds & Swaithe were members, while other sales were negotiated directly from the colliery office.

At only a short distance from the colliery lay the Worsbrough Dale gunpowder mills. The works were opened in the 1840s and are shown on the six inch ordnance survey map of 1850-51; they were owned by John Shortridge and Charles Wright and by 1861 were one of only two gunpowder mills in the whole of the West Riding. A new site lease was signed in June 1880 and in 1883 Henry Smith was a proprietor and managing partner. By 1904 the mills were worked by Kynock Ltd and were now the only gunpowder mills in the West Riding. By 1922 and 1927 Nobel's Explosive Co Ltd had the works, with a magazine keeper there. The works had closed by 1936.

The Barnsley Bed coal got at Edmunds Main was of the very best quality and was known to be 'harder than any other Colliery in the country', bringing a sale price better than those got at Wombwell Main or indeed at Swaithe Main. In 1885 the colliery supplied best hard steam coal at 6s 3d a ton to the Manchester, Sheffield & Lincolnshire Railway.

Benjamin Wilson, manager since *c.*1876, was ill in 1883 and soon to die. His thirty-seven-year-old son took over during his father's incapacity, having apparently worked under his father for three years at Darfield Main, and then as a certificated manager at one colliery for six years and at another for twenty months. But he was not to be appointed as his father's successor, having quarrelled with one of the major officials. The post was filled in 1884 by Henry Edward Gregory at £250 a year plus a house, rent and coals, with three months' notice on each side. Gregory had been at Hoyland Silkstone Colliery.

Hubert St John Durnford was the last full-time manager of the Swaithe and Edmunds collieries, from 1888 to 1892. A single man of only twenty-eight, Dunford was the son of a clergyman, a Cambridge MA, who was then Master of Eton and Fellow of the College. Hubert himself attended Eton. He took his first manager's certificate in 1881 and served his time, probably under articles, with George Walker at Wharncliffe Silkstone Colliery, remaining there for four years from the age of seventeen, the last few months as a deputy. He then moved to Nunnery Colliery, near Sheffield, where he remained for just six months, moving on to Earl Fitzwilliam's New Stubbin colliery in 1881, where he was under manager. He left there in 1886, to go to one of John Brown's pits at Aldwarke Main, near Rotherham, working under the great colliery manager, C E Rhodes, prior to taking the Edmunds/Swaithe position.

The colliery partnership was facing important economic and geological problems by 1890, facing the working out of the principal, Barnsley Seam, and the consequent need to work thinner seams or close. A trial sinking to the Thin Coal at Edmunds Main was made in early 1890 and the equipment for opening up production ordered – a Schiele fan from the United Engineering Company of Manchester, steam pipes from the Union Foundry of Barnsley, and metal window frames from Qualter Halls of Barnsley. A second hand winding engine was also required, along with timber for the corves and new safety lamps. The Thin Coal was reached in January 1890, the seam 2ft 6in in thickness. Working began by April and by July 130 tons a week was being extracted. However, such thin-coal workings were not always successful: in October 1890 there were 120 sets of colliers' tools in the Thin Seam, but a year later only 109. In June 1891 the Thin Seam employing just thirty men and boys at Swaithe Main was abandoned, although workings continued at Edmunds. Total production decreased from 4,000 tons per week in 1889 to 2,000 tons in 1891, but costs were also increasing. Durnford envisaged the company being reduced to what he described in his letter book as a 'muck pit'. Durnford continued to report, fortnightly, to Charles Bartholomew, shrewd as ever though now in his eighties and still a managing partner at Wombwell Main.

The early 1890s was a difficult period in the coal industry, with (locally) troubles culminating in the great strike of 1893, the Massacre at Featherstone and other disturbances in West and South Yorkshire. The situation for Edmunds and Swaithe was made worse by the imminent working out of the best coal and in September 1890 Edmunds Main was being dismantled. The state of the coal trade obviously affected wages and Durnford refers to both the difficulty of selling house coal and the necessity of temporarily closing down the coke kilns at Swaithe. In November Durnford, newly married, was given three months' notice of dismissal, principally because the collieries were worked out and managerial services could be provided by Arthur Tyas, son of one of the managing partners. He applied for a number of posts, unsuccessfully, but accepting an offer of a temporary position as a certified manager at Wharncliffe Silkstone Colliery. Eventually, by 1905, Durnford joined Corbett & Wood of Wharncliffe Chambers, Sheffield.

Durnford was succeeded as manager at Swaithe by William Tate, who may have been part-time. Tate had been trained at Cramlington Collieries in Northumberland and had been manager at Monk Bretton for nearly four years and then manager/agent at the West Ardsley Collieries at Tingley, near Leeds.

Closure was to come in September 1896, the remaining miners largely older men. The original proprietors were now either dead or very old men: Mitchell had died in 1876, John Tyas in 1895 and Bartholomew earlier that year. Tyas's death may have been a principal factor leading to the remaining partners – Tyas's two sons and Bartholomew junior – to decide only a few months later to cease working coal.

The Barnsley Bed and other seams were nearing exhaustion, the main leases nearing termination, and the cost of deeper sinkings would involve new leases and the sinking of new shafts. Water difficulties had been continuing. In 1889, pumping at Swaithe was said to cost £2,500. Edmunds had closed in the late 1880s and production at Swaithe had ceased.

In 1892 Bartholomew wrote that he would be willing to accept half of the price named by Ben Rylands, the Barnsley glass bottle manufacturer and colliery owner, as the sum he was willing to pay for Edmunds and Swaithe, but no sale was agreed. Closure came in 1896. The Barnsley Bed workings were abandoned in June 1896 and the Beamshaw Thin and Newhill workings in September of the same year. The coke ovens were kept at work, using bought-in coal, and the hiring of the company's coal wagons continued. Coke continued to be produced at the Swaithe ovens until the first half of 1908, having been then recently run down. In 1900 a new coal lease was taken and the concern was re-registered as the Swaithe Main Co Ltd, with a modest capital of £6,250 in £1 shares, but the move was later described as 'abortive'. In September 1908 the coke ovens were closed and C J Tyas was not prepared to risk further speculation regarding working the coal.

Negotiations began as to the disposal of the Gaskell lease to Stringers of Clayton West, colliery owners, and C E Stringer junior was consulted on the matter but in December 1910 the Gaskell lease was surrended and the coking plant sold. By January, 1911 the company had 'ceased to carry on business and will soon be wound up', and it was to be in December of that year that the winding-up meeting was held at Wombwell Main Colliery. What had been described as the concern – along with Joseph Mitchell's other interests – to which Worsbrough Dale was 'mainly indebted for its prosperity', had gone.

Notes

1. A more detailed essay on this subject – based on the Edmunds and Swaithe Collieries MSS – can be found at the writer's Local History Study Centre at Wakefield.

8. A SHORT LIFE AND A LONG DEATH: THE DEARNE DISTRICT LIGHT RAILWAYS

by Richard Buckley

THE DEARNE VALLEY lies roughly between Barnsley and Swinton in what has always been something of a border territory: between the Pennines and flatter land around Doncaster, between the exposed coalfields of the Barnsley area and the concealed coalfield further east, and between the heavily built-up South Yorkshire conurbation of Sheffield/Rotherham and the more sparsely populated and fertile farmlands on the magnesian limestone ridge on its further edge. Local government has also added its divisions, firstly between the small Urban Districts (UDCs) of Bolton, Darfield, Wombwell, Wath and Thurnscoe and today between the larger units of Barnsley and Rotherham. Partly as a result of all this, the valley has never been an important through route; there are more direct ways of getting to larger places. However, the development of coal mining meant that transport out of the valley became increasingly important. To this end, the Dearne and Dove Canal was constructed from 1793 to 1804 between the River Don and Barnsley, together with two branches to Elsecar and Worsbrough.[1] As a result of this and other transport improvements, together with technical progress, the South Yorkshire Coalfield expanded rapidly during the next century. There were 81 collieries in 1855 and 108 in 1870 (Manvers Main, near Wath, opened that same year). At the same time, the centre of gravity of the industry shifted east, from Barnsley towards Rotherham and Doncaster, meaning that by the end of the century many of the largest mines were in the Dearne valley.[2] This further expansion was both fuelled by and attracted the railway companies, of which five had lines in the area. The Great Central was the only one to run right along the valley, between Barnsley and Mexborough. The Midland served Barnsley and Wombwell (and still does), the Hull & Barnsley had a branch via Thurnscoe to Wath and the Dearne Valley Railway skirted the area on its way from Wakefield to Edlington (near Doncaster) and had a halt at Goldthorpe. The last two were quite clearly built to exploit the coal traffic and in all cases passengers were a secondary consideration. The first three companies all had stations at Wath, but they were widely separated

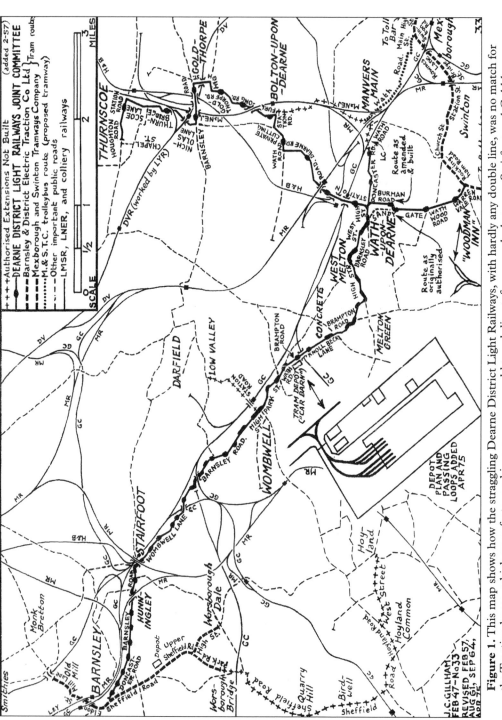

Figure 1. This map shows how the straggling Dearne District Light Railways, with hardly any double line, was no match for the Traction buses, which were faster and in many cases could travel direct, for example, between Stairfoot and Goldthorpe.

and of no help to through passengers.[3] The Midland and North Eastern Railways had a joint line serving Bolton (the only other original station in the area still to be open), but this was not much use for people wanting to travel to Wath.[4] Local opinion was forthright! It was said of (the former) Court House station in Barnsley that 'the only thing' the railway companies 'will do is to paint it occasionally, otherwise it may some day fall to pieces altogether'.[5] A local solicitor added that 'train and station accommodation on the Great Central (nicknamed by another witness the 'Gentle Crawler'![6]) is about as bad for passengers as can be well conceived.' (Figure 1).

Interestingly, the lawyer mentioned that in 1906 he had been asked by a London firm to do the legal work for a Wath to Barnsley tramway, which would have had several branches, including one up to Darfield.[7] This was one of several abortive schemes for a tramway in the area, probably inspired by the fact that lines had been projected and were eventually opened at either end of the valley, the Barnsley & District towards the end of 1902 and the Mexborough & Swinton in 1907,[8] both private enterprise concerns, unlike the future Dearne District. In May 1913, however, the Barnsley company, which was part of the much larger British Electric Traction (BET) group, introduced a motor bus service to Wombwell and this was, in their opinion, 'the best travelling facility for this district'. Contemporary opinion was divided on the merits of omnibuses, with the traditional view being that they were all right for 'opening up new districts' or for testing the traffic, but that a tramway would be necessary in the long run. The four local Urban Districts of Bolton, Goldthorpe, Wath and Wombwell chose to follow this orthodoxy, very largely due to the persuasive argument of the consulting engineer for the scheme, Stephen Sellon[9] (whose firm, of course, stood to profit from the construction of the tramway and not at all from the continuance of private enterprise bus services). The Light Railway Commissioners[10] rejected most of the arguments of the bus and railway companies and authorised the construction of the Dearne District Light Railways (DDLR) at the close of their 1914 Inquiry.

The lines as authorised were not as they were eventually built, and the details of the subsequent legal manoeuvres and of the construction period are too complex to discuss here. Suffice to say that the DDLR almost certainly had the longest period ever (at least until the reintroduction of tramways towards the end of the last century) between authorisation and opening, because it was ten

Figure 2. Car 6, smartly finished in the original livery of bright red and white, stands on the track fan in the car barn yard. *Author's collection*

years before the main line between Barnsley and Thurnscoe via Wombwell, Wath and Goldthorpe opened on 14 July 1924 (Figure 2). The branch from Wath to Manvers Main opened on the same day and was followed later by a second branch to the *Woodman Inn*, Swinton.[11] The delay was mostly due to the intervention of the First World War, but was also as a result of almost endless legal proceedings, the continued opposition of other transport firms and the prevarication of some of the local councils.

Operation

The DDLR had a number of features of interest. It was the last complete street tramway opened in the UK.[12] Its circuitous route was laid almost entirely in the roads, but it did have one section of private track in Bolton-upon-Dearne, built to avoid an awkward road junction. Many of the staff came from the Paisley system in Scotland, which had recently been taken over by Glasgow Corporation. This included the General Manager, Major Fred Coutts, and a number of the drivers (known as motormen) of whom there were not, of course, many in the Dearne area.[13] The Manager resigned fairly early upon his appointment to a new post, but was taken ill and died in March 1925 before he could move; his son, Ronald, was appointed to succeed him. The depot, always known in American parlance as the Car Barns, was built on a rather isolated site between Wombwell and West Melton. Because of this, and also because of the influx of new employees, it was decided to build a 'company' housing estate next

Figure 3. Car 5, in High Street, Wath, on the 'main line' service out to Thurnscoe, passing a horse drawn cart on one of the relatively few pieces of double track on the system. *Rotherham Metropolitan Borough Council, Libraries and Information Services, Archives and Local Studies Section*

to it, a rather uncommon arrangement.[14] Nearby was the only major civil engineering feature on the line, an overbridge over a colliery railway. The Light Railway Commissioners had insisted this was built instead of relying on a level crossing (Figure 3).

At two points the DDLR reached the metals of other tramways, at Doncaster Road (the Alhambra), Barnsley and at the *Woodman Inn*, Swinton. Junctions were authorised with, respectively, the Barnsley & District and the Mexborough & Swinton lines.[15] Had both been built, the DDLR could have become a link in a network of inter-urban tramways connecting Barnsley with Swinton, Rotherham and Sheffield. However, although the junction at the *Woodman Inn* was

Figure 4. Car 18 outward bound in High Street, Wombwell, possibly on an inaugural run, given the amount of interest shown in proceedings by the local children. *Author's collection*

laid, it was hardly ever used. At an early date one of the DDLR cars, which were long single-deckers, was tried out on the line towards Rawmarsh. However, the dip at the bottom of (the old) Warren Vale Road caused it to 'ground', which brought an immediate end to the experiment.[16] Several years later, on Tuesday 10 April 1928, an hourly service began between Wath and Rotherham. This obviously used the shorter company cars, which were double-deck. At least one was kept overnight at the car barns, so during that time double-deck trams ran through as far as Wombwell. DDLR crews ran the whole *Woodman* service with company cars, but the hourly through car was taken on by a Mexborough crew. Planned for a month,[17] for some reason the trial was terminated by the DDLR side in only a week.[18] The Barnsley junction was never put in. Normal services were operated as a 'main line' from Barnsley to Thurnscoe via Wombwell, Wath and Goldthorpe (Figure 4). The two branches were operated as shuttle services, starting from West Melton and running respectively to Manvers and the *Woodman*.

Financially, the DDLR was a disaster, a fact of which the local councillors had been well warned before the line was built. Mr Chivers of the BET said at the 1914 Inquiry that, were the line 'ever constructed and worked, I have no hesitation in saying... it will be worked at a loss, and a very considerable loss too.'[19] Innocents amongst wolves, these well-meaning men, desiring only the best for their communities, were (in the writer's opinion) taken for a ride by city-slickers who could see the opportunity of taking profit before the consequences of their advice became too obvious. Sellon was wildely optimistic in his evidence. He claimed, for example, that the DDLR would take about two and a half times the revenue of the existing Barnsley tramway and carry double the passengers on the Mexborough line,[20] whilst it was well known (and fairly obvious) that tramways with a lot of line as compared to population were much more likely to under perform. It is true that the undertaking returned a working surplus until 1929-30 (except for the year of the General Strike), but thereafter there was a regular loss on current account. The real killer was the loan charges on the construction costs, which had been much higher after the war than they would have been previously. From 1928 the debt payments averaged around £18-19,000, always wiping out any profit and, in the final year, leaving the authorities with a deficit of £23,092 to cover from the rates.[21] At the time, this was a large sum, especially for four quite small townships, and it was an insupportable burden. So, on 30 September 1933, after barely nine years of service, the trams were replaced by the buses of the competing Yorkshire Traction Company (as the former Barnsley tramway operator had become).

The Struggle to Live... and Afterlife
The most interesting aspect of the DDLR's short history is the effort made by the Joint Committee of the four authorities to compete or come to a *modus vivendi* with their main competitor. This was not the railways, despite their determined resistance to the plans for a light railway before the War. Although an extreme example, an amusing exchange at the Inquiry reveals the reason why; the railways weren't carrying much traffic on their local lines anyway. Counsel for the Hull & Barnsley Railway complained that the tramway would abstract passengers, and already some trains were running with only one or two passengers. Chairman: 'So it would be a good thing for you if you were run off the line altogether?' Counsel: 'Not altogether!'[22] The difficulty lay with the burgeoning number of bus operators, many of which were very small affairs, though some, such as Burrows (still remembered locally) were larger. Most of the smaller concerns were taken over in time by the Traction Company, and it is the latter which was the DDLR's nemesis.

The Barnsley & District Electric Traction Company, as it was then,

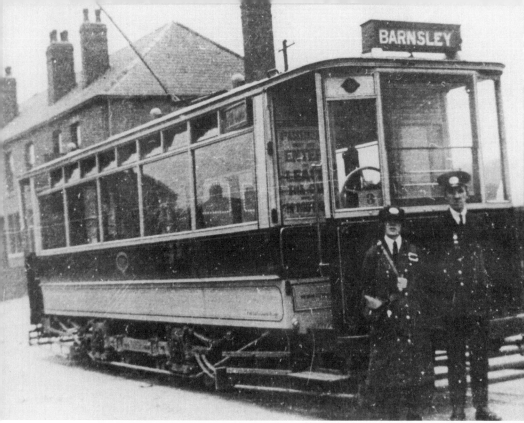

Figure 5. The crew pose at the front of their Barnsley-bound car, possibly at Thurnscoe terminus. The DDLR always employed conductresses so as to provide female employment in an area where most work was for men. The large wheel on the rather confined driving platform was for the hand brake.
Author's collection

started bus operations in 1913. After the War there were still only seventeen vehicles in the fleet and around five services, but within a decade the fleet had grown to 142 buses serving 164 towns and villages.[23] The DDLR was thus only a small area within the Company's sphere of operation and virtually the whole of its route was covered by Traction buses. Nevertheless, the Company was not going to ignore this threat to its 'home turf' and took a firm line from the start. 'If you lower your fares, we shall lower ours,' the Chairman (L M Myers) said in 1925, whilst at the same time recommending the Committee 'not [to] spend another penny on tramways, their day is past.'[24]

The DDLR tried four tactics to accommodate itself to or to resist its larger neighbour (Figure 5). These were, in rough chronological order, co-ordination and protection; out-and-out competition; pooling; and finally, surrender. Co-ordination meant an attempt to run what would nowadays be called an integrated service, or at least one where trams and buses were not running at the same times.

Local authorities at that period did have the right to licence buses in their areas and Wombwell UDC attempted to use its powers in 1924 to refuse licences for direct services to Barnsley, leaving bus operators only with the task of 'feeding' the tramway.[25] However, the Traction Company and other larger independent firms appealed to the Minister of Transport, who would not support the refusal of the licences, but did enforce an arrangement whereby all the bus companies had to agree to the co-ordination of timetables and to the imposition of a protective fare. That is, bus fares were to be levied at three pence (just over 1p) over each one penny fare stage on the tramway. The agreement was to last for one year,[26] and was a fairly significant achievement on the part of the Committee.

The agreement was not renewed, however, and a policy of competition with the bus company was put in its place. Early in 1927 a bold and desperate move was taken to attract passengers to the municipal trams by cutting fares drastically from the normal rate of one pence per mile to a maximum of only three pence per journey.[27] This reduction was, of course, immediately matched by the Traction Company, who also withdrew the former protective fares; there was, they said, no apparent diminution in revenue.[28] The DDLR also made an attempt to compete in terms of comfort. It was not that their trams were old, but they were built to a traditional design and lacked the pneumatic tyres and cushioned and sprung seats of the more modern buses. So in 1926 it was decided to modernise one car experimentally by replacing the long wooden benches which ran the full length of the saloon with cross-seating. Short lengths of the old seats were left at each end for workmen in dirty clothes,[29] but the rest was replaced by 'swing back' seats of the normal tramway pattern, still with wooden backs, but now with the luxury of cushions(Figure 6). Brighter lighting and a white ceiling gave a much more cheerful impression too. Following this success, it was decided to convert further cars, though in the end the money ran out, and only four were done.[30] The low fares obviously *did* have a positive effect on ridership, for the financial year 1927-28 produced the highest working surplus in the line's existence and also a lower deficit after loan charges than was ever achieved again.[31] However, there was still no possibility of breaking even and the DDLR had to go back to the Traction Company cap in hand and re-negotiate the co-ordination and protection agreement, somewhat to their disadvantage, as the excess bus fare was now reduced to only one penny.[32]

Stage three of this fraught relationship was the concept of pooling,

Figure 6. The modernised saloon car 27, showing the comfortable cross seating and bright ceiling, all of which must have given a good impression to intending passengers. This was the last of the four cars to be modernised, though even if funds had been available only the final five cars delivered were suitable for adaptation. *Author's collection*

the idea being that in their joint area the DDLR and the Company would run approximately the same mileage and pool the receipts, each party to receive half after certain expenses had been met. Both would co-operate to reduce or eliminate competition from other smaller bus companies, either by licensing control (the authorities) or by buying them out (the company). The negotiations to achieve this were bitterly contested and were characterised by regular recourse to m'learned friends and by brinkmanship on both sides. Initially, Ronald Coutts said that 'not under any circumstances can I see any advantage to the Joint Committee under the proposed pooling arrangements',[33] the problem being that not enough bus receipts would have gone in the pool. Many of the councillors were not keen on a rapprochement between municipal and private enterprise either; it was 'impossible to mix oil with water', said one.[34] Such an agreement was anyway thought by the Ministry of Transport to be *ultra vires* and an Act would have to be sought to permit it. The Committee were, however, allowed to proceed as long as no payments were made by them before the Act was passed. Pooling was due to begin on Monday, 8 April 1929, but the day before the Company suddenly pulled out on instructions from head office in London because of fears that monies due would not be paid. Legal opinion was sought, but in the event the pool started on 22 April without waiting for a response.[35] The legal situation proving as the Minister had thought, the DDLR drew up a Bill to be deposited by 17 December, but in this case Wombwell Council withdrew its support, also at the last minute, because they wanted a vigourous effort to speed up the trams and solicit public support.[36] A last hope was to get the powers incorporated in the *Road Traffic Act* then going through Parliament, but this drew the frosty response from the Ministry that 'they were not in a position to do anything more for the Committee'.[37] Despite the lack of a legal basis, the pool was continued until closure, the mileage being arranged so that money was always due from the Company and not vice versa.[38] Unfortunately, despite the hopes invested in it, the arrangement was if anything disadvantageous to the DDLR. Instead of falling as competition was reduced, mileage run actually rose, whilst revenue fell (Figure 7), albeit slowly.[39] Meanwhile, local

Figure 7. Car 24 at the car barns, and in a later livery without the white lower (or rocker) panels; colour schemes were often simplified on tramways in order to save money on maintenance. The spring loaded reel on the dash beside the headlamp was designed to keep the trolley rope taut; at that time it was quite an innovative feature, later more commonly found on trolleybuses. The upper row of small windows, known as quarter lights, could be opened to provide ventilation; it was evidently thought that standing passengers on the DDLR did not need to see out of them, because the glass was an opaque orange. *Author's collection*

people realised that it no longer mattered which form of transport they used.[40] As Mr Robinson, the Traction Company's General Manager from 1928, said: 'if passengers are going to ride on the tram they will have to be forced to do so, especially in view of the fast moving vehicles of the Traction Company.'[41] As the balance owed by the Traction Company rose they used this as a weapon in their campaign to force the DDLR to sell up. Robinson again: 'we shall fight to the last gate', and if there is no agreement, the pool receipts will not be paid over.[42]

That presaged the fourth and final phase in the battle: surrender. County Alderman George Probert, a key member and later Chairman of the Joint Committee, said at the meeting with Robinson that 'we have got to the end of our tether'. Sykes has an excellent summary of the options open to them at the beginning of the 1930s: to carry on as they were; to double the track; to replace trams by buses or trollybuses (either their own or as an extension of those now run by the Mexborough & Swinton Company); to abandon the light railways without replacement; or, finally, to sell out to the Yorkshire Traction Company, either outright or as nominal partners in the continuing services.[43] This final option was the one chosen. The Company guaranteed a fixed payment of £3,000 p.a. for the first five years and £2,000 thereafter; if higher profits were earned, they would be divided 50:50. 'Profits' were defined as the balance after operating costs of 10.125 pence (about 4p) had been subtracted, that figure would vary only with changes in the price of fuel and tyres.[44] Even after closure, therefore, the Joint Committee continued a kind of shadow existence as a sleeping partner in the pool area bus services until the annual loan payments on the light railway were finally extinguished on 4 May 1966.[45]

Upon closure, everything was put up for sale. Some of the assets, such as the car barn, were included in the Agreement with Yorkshire Traction. But they naturally did not require any of the vehicles. Since trams were going out of fashion everywhere in the country, not many found a buyer. Four cars went to Lytham St Annes and ran there (and over the still-existing Blackpool tramway) until 1937. Another five, including the four modernised ones, were purchased by a tramway company in Falkirk, where they had to be shortened and adapted for four foot gauge track, but these lasted only until 1936.[46] One car body ended up in a garden in Wath and another, which is still there, found a new use as a bungalow at Langsett, just beyond Stocksbridge, and forms virtually the last physical reminder of the Quixotic little municipal

Figure 8. Almost certainly this is the last relic of the DDLR, a car body, which has been standing in a field at Langsett for about 70 years since the line closed in 1933. Other bodies were sold off as garden sheds or storage units, but no others are known to have survived. *Richard Buckley*

enterprise (Figure 8).

So, as is usually the case in the real world, Goliath had triumphed over the boy David. And so it seemed to be. The four authorities' shares of the annual loan charges were roughly £7,155 for Wombwell, £4,440 for Wath, £4,465 for Bolton and £1,940 for Thurnscoe.[47] £3,000 p.a. and later only £2,000 wasn't going far against such liabilities, though it was still better than the previous situation when councils had been meeting working losses as well.

However, history, or more properly the future, has an endless ability to surprise. Far from falling, the payments to the DDLR rose steadily, from the final guaranteed minimum payment of £3,000 in 1938 to £4,246 in the following year, then to £17,536 in 1944 and finally to £21,968 in 1949. Over those same four financial years the balance of receipts in the Dearne area retained by Yorkshire Traction fell inexorably from a base of £13,545, first marginally to £13,522, and then more steeply to £8,226 and in the last year to a loss of £2,773. How had this state of affairs come about? The problem was that bus operating costs had risen fast during the war years and the later 1940s, almost doubling from 7.75 pence (about 3p) per bus mile in 1939 to 14.35 (6p) a decade later. The Catch 22 was that costs chargeable under the Agreement had hardly risen at all and even by 1949 were only 10.69 pence (just over 4p) per bus mile. The company's earnings were barely more than their running costs anyway by then, but after subtracting these wholly artificial 'costs' from gross earnings, the account with the Councils showed a nominal profit, half of which had to be paid over. In the Bolton area alone, therefore, the Company paid £7,788 in 1949, leaving itself to meet a loss of £2,685.[48] 'The great mistake which was made from our (the Company's) standpoint was that the Agreement covering a period of thirty-three years should only provide for variation of the basic figure to the limited extent of the rise or fall of fuel and tyres... No account is taken of the tremendous increase in labour charges, and practically every commodity we use, nor of the increased cost of rolling stock.'[49] This report continued by urging the renegotiation of the Agreement, but recognising that the Councils were not legally bound to do this, tacitly admitted that fares might have to be increased sharply to cover the losses, even though this would only result in yet higher payments to the Joint Committee, as much as £30,000, 'a truly exorbitant figure'.[50]

At this point, the records run out, so it is not known whether or not the Agreement was renegotiated or whether the payments continued to be made until its expiry. However it was, it seems clear enough that if one slings rocks at a giant long enough, eventually he falls over! The DDLR was a long time a'dying, and in the process it turned what seemed its out-and-out defeat into something of a Pyrric victory for its rival. 'Tracky' has survived worse things, however, including nationalisation and privatisation, and is still as much a part of the life of many Barnsley and Dearne people as it was very nearly a century ago, when it first began running trams and then buses from its Sheffield Road depot.

Notes and References

1. C Hadfield, *The Canals of Yorkshire & North East England*,2 , Newton Abbot, 1973, pp.282-5.
2. C D B Gray, 'The South Yorkshire Coalfield', in J.Benson & R.G. Neville (eds), *Studies in the Yorkshire Coal Industry*, Manchester, 1976, pp.35-7.
3. The main sources for this article are the extraordinarily copious records of the DDLR formerly held in the South Yorkshire Record Office (now Sheffield Archives). Documents cited are from this source unless otherwise stated and are identified by archive reference 'number', by name (both abbreviated on subsequent mentions) and finally by date and/or page. Railway services are described in 8/UD/28/1, Light Railway Commissioners' Inquiry, Barnsley, 24 February 1914, Brief for Applicants, pp.6-7.
4. 28/3., Minutes of Proceedings of Light Railway Commissioners Inquiry 1914, p.380.
5. Brief, p.8.
6. 28/12, Further Witness Statements to the Inquiry, Wm Beardsall's evidence, p.2.
7. 28/10, Miscellaneous Witness Statements to the Inquiry on 21 July 1914, pp.2-3.
8. W H Bett & J C Gilham(ed. J H Price), *The Tramways of South Yorkshire and Humberside* (n.d.), pp.3 & 5.
9. Proceedings, pp.165, 169, 182, 630 & 647.
10. The line was promoted under the 1896 *Light Railways Act*, which came to be used almost entirely for tramway schemes due to the less onerous regulations as compared to the 1870 *Tramways Act*; the DDLR was, however, a street tramway in all but name.
11. 28/544, Minutes of the Joint Committee 30 August 1922 - 15 December 1932, pp. 66-67 & 88; the committee included representatives of Bolton, Wath, Wombwell and Thurnscoe UDCs.
12. Bett & Gilham, South Yorkshire Tramways, p.4; the last, of course, prior to the recent crop of new tramways, such as the South Yorkshire Supertram.
13. A S Denton, *DDLR The Story of the Dearne District Light Railways and Competitors,* Bromley Common, 1980, p.10; this excellent brief history was written by the son of a DDLR motorman and covers all the essential facts.
14. Joint Committee Minutes, pp.14, 49, 105, 118 & 121.
15. 28/14, Dearne District Light Railways Order 1915.
16. C C Hall, 'A History of the Barnsley, Dearne, Mexborough & Rotherham Tramway Conurbation', Part 2, in *Tramway Review* 7:56, 1968, p.175.
17. 28/484/Z1/1, Note on Through Service, pp.1-2.
18. Joint Committee Minutes, 19 April 1928 (later minutes lack page numbers).
19. Proceedings, p.634.
20. *Ibid.*, pp.265 & 267.
21. All the figures are found in 28/558-67, Financial Statements of Revenue Charges, passim.
22. Inquiry, p.452.
23. J A Sykes, *Yorkshire Traction*, Barnsley, 1982, pp.12 & 18; this excellent book takes the detailed story only up to 1945, but has a full fleet list.
24. Joint Committee Minutes, 23 February 1925.
25. 1/17, Wombwell UDC Minutes, Highways & Buildings Committee, 16 September 1924, pp.305-6.
26. Joint Committee Minutes, 17 December 1925.
27. *Ibid.*, 21 February 1927.
28. The records of Yorkshire Traction and its predecessors were consulted at Sheffield Road, Barnsley in the early 1980s when it was part of the National Bus Company, to whom the papers were due to be returned; their current whereabouts is not known. Most records prior to 1929 were destroyed in a fire, except for a few minute books held at BET headquarters in London. This reference is to Barnsley & District Electric Traction Co., Minute Book 2,3 May 1927.
29. Possibly the persons referred to in a notice inside the cars which ran something like this: 'Gentlemen will not spit; others should not'.
30. 28/546, DDLR Works Committee Minutes, 7 July 1926 and Denton, *DDLR*, p.23; Denton doesn't make it clear that the fare cuts and car improvements were made early in the life of the tramway.
31. 28/604, Statement of Revenue Charges allocated to the...Authorities.
32. Joint Committee Minutes, 14 July 1927.
33. *Ibid.*, 17 December 1928.
34. *Ibid.*, 7 April 1929.
35. *Ibid.*, 17 January, 21 February, 7 & 18 April 1929.
36. Clerk's Reports (bound with Minutes) and Minutes (Local Authorities Conference), both 19 December 1928.

37. Clerk's Reports, 10 December 1931.

38. 28/534. Brief for the Yorkshire Traction Company, 3 May 1933, p.6.

39. Ministry of Transport Returns for Street and Road Tramways, Dearne District.

40. Clerk's Reports, 10 December 1931.

41. Joint Committee Minutes, Special Sub-Committee, 5 February 1930.

42. 28/609, Miscellaneous Papers, Meeting of Members...with Yorkshire Traction Company, 20 May 1931.

43. Sykes, *Yorkshire Traction*, p.26.

44. Miscellaneous Papers, Letter from the Secretary to the...Company, 9 July 1932. The Company had wanted to include wages, but this was turned down; see ibid., Negotiations with the...Company, 8 July 1932.

45. 28/510, Agreement as to the Abandonment of Light Railways, 17 November 1932, p.2.

46. Denton, p.24.

47. Miscellaneous Papers, Evidence of J L Hawksworth, p.8.

48. *The Yorkshire Traction Company Ltd, Dearne District Operation* (n.d., but late 1950) and Statement in respect of services operating in Bolton-upon-Dearne Area (1949).

49. *Yorkshire Traction Company*, [A report on the] *Dearne District Light Railway* (n.d. but evidently late 1950), pp.2 & 3.

50. *Ibid.*, pp.4-5.

9. EXTRACTS FROM ROYSTON SECONDARY SCHOOL LOG BOOKS, 1934-1945

by John Broom

ROYSTON BOYS' SECONDARY SCHOOL and Royston Girls' Secondary School were opened in 1934 in response to a number of factors. The school leaving age for children had been raised to eleven in 1891 and twelve in 1899. The *Fisher's Education Act* of 1918 raised this to fourteen and the *Hadow Report* of 1926 recommended turning the senior sections of elementary schools into separate secondary schools and raising the leaving age to fifteen. Although the latter was not achieved until *Butler's Education Act* of 1944, the rising numbers of older children in schools, and the widening age range of pupils from five to fourteen meant that many authorities decided that a two-phase education system was desirable.

Figure 1. Most of these successful Royston Council School footballers, winners of the prestigious Felkirk Cup in season 1932-33, would soon be transferring to the new Royston Secondary School. The boys are, back row (left to right): Whitehouse, Stephens, Sheldon, Hill and Hinchmore; and seated: Hindmarsh, Sleight, Hughes, Hayward, Woods, Smart and Harris. *Brian Elliott Collection*

The early 1930s in Royston saw the development of much new housing, including areas around Park View, Newtown Avenue and West End Crescent. The resulting influx of children of secondary school age meant that the existing two schools, Royston National School (the Church School) and Royston Council School (Parkside School) could no longer cope with the increasing numbers (Figure 1). As a result a decision was taken to build two new schools, one for the boys and one for the girls as an extension of the existing Council School on Midland Road (demolished in 1985).

The School Log Books
The log books currently housed in the archives of Royston High School consist of four volumes:

Royston Boys' School, September 1934 to March 1952
Royston Boys' School, April 1952 to July 1965
Royston Girls' School, September 1934 to July 1965
Royston Modern School, September 1965 to July 1978

From 1934, the Heads of both the Boys' and Girls' schools were required under Schedule IV of the *Education Code* to keep a regular record of school events:

Every school must have:-

(a) A Diary or Log Book which should be a bare record of the events which constitute the history of the school. The Log Book should be stoutly bound and contain not less than 200 ruled pages. It must be kept at the school under the care of the Head Teacher. He should enter in it, from time to time, such events as the introduction of new books, apparatus, or courses of instruction, any plan of lessons approved by the board, the visits of managers, absence, illness, or failure of duty in the part of any school staff, or any special circumstance affecting the school that may, for the sake of future reference or for any other reason, deserve to be recorded.

The Log Books constitute a fascinating record of changing times in education and hint at wider changes in social attitudes which reflect on the life of the school which has served children of secondary school age in Royston for the last sixty-three years. The Log Book of the Boys' School contains a wider range of evidence than does that of the Girls' School, which explains the weighting in favour of Mr Laycock's entries in the following excerpts. An attempt to put the content of these log books into their wider context in the life of the school and the village will be the subject of a future study. What follows is selected excerpts from the school log books which may be of interest to the reader.

1934-1935

Aug 29th
(Boys)

I, George F. Laycock opened this new school.

Staff:

George F. Laycock	*Head Master*
Gwilym Jones CA	*(History & English)*
John V. Edmonds (BSc)	*(Science & Maths)*
Jno. Wm. Davy CA	*(Art & Maths)*
Arnold Green CA	*(Geog & Art)*
Thos. H. Arundel	*(Music & P.T.)*
Ronald Southern CA	*(Woodwork)*
Arth. H. Wilson BA	*(English)*
Alfd. Martin CA	
James Evans City & G	*(Metalwork)*

Note the absence of Languages, whether classics or modern and a specialist R E master. This was a very young and inexperienced staff (Figures 2-3), only the Head and Mr Jones having had more than three years' teaching experience at the time.

In accordance with regulations have delegated power to inflict corporal punishment to Mr. Jones, Mr. Arundel, Mr. Edmonds, Mr. Green, Mr. Southern and Mr. Davy.

Royston Boys' School had 348 boys on roll, split into 8 forms ranging from 36 pupils up to 55 pupils in Class IIIA. The boys were

Figure 2. A c.1934 photograph showing the new staff of Royston Senior Boys' School. They are, standing (left to right): Thomas H Arundel, R Murdock, James Evans, Alfred Martin, John W Davy and Arthur H Wilson.
Seated: John V Edmonds, Gwilym Jones, George F Laycock (Head Master), Ronald Southern and Arnold Green. *H. Jones*

Figure 3. Another early staff photograph. Standing (left to right): Ronald Southern, -?-, John W Davy, Gwilym Jones, -?-. Seated: Arnold Green, Arthur H Wilson and (?). The school caretaker is standing, slightly apart from the teaching staff. *Brian Elliott Collection*

Figure 4. A later (c.1957) photograph of the long-serving Head Mistress, Miss F. Parker and the school prefects of Royston Senior Girls' School. *M Elstone*

aged between eleven and fourteen.

The Girls' School at the time of opening welcomed 270 pupils split into 7 classes with between 35 and 40 girls per class. There were 'A' and 'B' classes based on age and a 'C' stream which contained pupils across the age range. 167 pupils came from Royston Council School Girls' Department, 44 from Royston Church School and 59 from Carlton Girls' School.

Aug 29th
(Girls)   *Staff*
            Head Teacher   *Florry Parker* (Figure 4)
                                  Rudd, Florence Lillian
                                  Washington, Annie Louisa
                                  Littlewood, Henrietta
                                  Pogson, Marian
                                  Cairns, Jemima Hall
                                  McBride, Catherine
                                  Hookins, Betsy Dorothea
                                  Travis, Dorothy

Saturday, 22 September 1934 saw the official opening of both schools by Sir Percy R Jackson LL.D, Chairman of the West Riding Education Committee (Figure 5). It was attended by Mr G A Griffiths, MP for Hemsworth, Captain H N Penlington, ex-President of the National Union of Teachers and Rev E F Walker MA, Vicar of Royston. The *National Anthem* was sung and a newspaper report (source unknown) is contained in Mr Laycock's Log Book:

Speaking at the opening of the new £21,000 Royston Senior School... Sir Percy Jackson... pleaded for a truer appreciation of three factors essential in a complete education, namely, faithfulness, common sense and cheerfulness. Captain H.N. Penlington... appealed for the co-operation of the parents, otherwise the labours of the teachers would be futile. The site of the new school consists of 5¹/₂ acres and the building consists of two separate blocks – one a boys' department with accommodation for 320 and a girls' department with accommodation for 360.

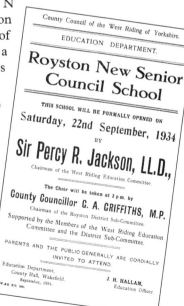

Figure 5. Printed Programme for the official opening of the 'Royston New Senior Council School', Saturday, 22 September 1934.
Royston High School Archives

Figure 6. Part of the original Boys' block, probably photographed in the 1950s, for *The Official Guide*, published by Royston Urban District Council, by which time the site was described as a 'Modern School' with separate departments for boys and girls. *Brian Elliott Collection*

Classrooms (Figure 6) must have been crowded, especially in the Boys' block which contained ten teaching areas only.

Oct 11th   *Closed school for Autumn break 1¹/₂ days.*
                  Allowed school football team to play staff from 11.00
                  to 11.40.

Nov 27th   <u>Royston Senior Council School</u>
                  "I have to inform you that the above named school
                  has now been recognised by the Board of Education as
                  a public elementary school as from 29 August 1934.
                  The School number will be 953 and accommodation will
                  be recognised for 280 scholars in the Senior Boys' Dept
                  (6x40 + 2x20) and 320 scholars in the Senior Girls'
                  Dept (7x40 + 2x20)" – Mr Gibbs – LEA.

Nov 29th   *Holiday. Royal Wedding, Duke of Kent, Princess Marina*

Free milk was distributed to needy pupils, even during holiday periods, by the Caretaker.

Every year, the Headteachers had to report to the Authority on their staff. Details were sent regarding years of service, wages and quality of teaching. A typical example from the time:

Mr Green   1yr 7mths 3 days   £177-13-0
Mr Green gives complete satisfaction. He is a good disciplinarian and in his subjects, Geography and Art, is doing very good work. His lessons always show careful preparation and thought.

Salaries at the time varied from £159 to £295 p.a. depending on length of service and qualifications.

Jan 17th	*Medical Inspection concluded. Following boys ordered Cod Liver Oil.*

Arthur Nicholson   Bernard Stallam
Richard York   Victor Jones
Jack Etheridge

Jan 23rd   *Mr Smith P.T. Organiser brought action films and Pathescope and showed to boys at 5.30 pm.*

Late January of 1935 saw the first reference to a tradition which remains strong in the school to the present day.

Jan 29th   *Held a meeting of boys who propose going on school outing and the unanimous choice was Edinburgh.*

The tradition of giving pupils gifts to celebrate royal events was obviously popular in the 1930s:

March 20th   *Received notice of 1 day's holiday for Silver Jubilee, also that each child over 11 to receive a fountain pen and each child under 11 to receive a pencil.*

April 8th   *Received notice that in celebration of the Silver Jubilee two days holiday viz. May 6th & 7th will be granted, also each child is to have a bank book with 1/- in it not withdrawable before 16 yrs of age.*

April 12 saw all teachers receive a pay cut of 5 per cent with no evident threat of industrial action.

May 6th   *Jubilee Day*
(Girls)   *11 am   Children listened to the Thanksgiving Service held in St Paul's Cathedral.*
              2.30 pm   paid a visit to the cinema.
              4.30 pm   Tea in the school. Received Jubilee mugs.

June 8th   *SCHOOL TRIP*
              81 boys made journey to Edinbro', leaving Royston at 1 am Edinburgh was reached 7.10.
              The boys visited Forth Bridge, Princes St. Zoo, Holyrood and the Castle and arrived home at 12.30 on June 9th.

Mr Laycock seems to have had little say in the appointment of his staff as the following example indicates:

July 18th   *Received intimation that Mr A Cannon 38 Church Street, Shoreditch, London EC2 has been appointed Metalwork Instructor to succeed Mr Evans.*

July 31st   *School Sports held in afternoon. School closed by*
                 permission of Education Committee.
                 The proceedings were very successful and the weather
                 ideal. The event was held in the Welfare Cricket Field
                 which is rented by the School Staff for School Cricket.
                 There were no prizes but marks were awarded to Houses:

Caxton (Blue)	*100*
Grenville (Green)	*60*
Ruskin (Red)	*44*
Priestley (White)	*35*

1935-36

The year started with the admission of boys from the local area and around the British Isles:

Sept 2nd   *Mr Avigdor Cannon of Shoreditch commenced duties as*
                Metalwork instructor.
                Admitted: 52 boys from Royston Junior Boys.
                       13 boys from Royston National School.
                       20 boys from Carlton Junior School.
                       boy from Bury.
                       boy from Domerail Co. Cork.

The practice of giving the pupils holidays for royal occasions continued:

Nov 1st   *Received notice of holiday Nov 6th Royal Wedding*
                (Duke of Gloucester).
                Received notice of holiday Nov 14th General Election.
Nov 6th   *School closed Royal Wedding.*

More day to day incidents are recorded, some in bizarre circumstances:

Nov 26th   *Joseph Perkins IC in pushing open a door cut his hand.*

Early January 1936, Mr Laycock sent off his annual reports on his staff, including the following testimony of which any teacher would be proud:

Southern, Ronald   *£224.0.0*   *4yrs 8mths*

     Mr Southern continues to do good work. He has charge of the Woodwork dept. and conducts it on sound education lines. He is thoroughly interested in all phases of school life and spares no effort to further the welfare of the boys, especially in summer sports and the organisation of the Annual Excursion.

Records were kept by both schools of milk issued during holidays:

Jan 6th (Girls)	*No. of bottles of free milk distributed over the holidays.*		
	Mon 23rd Dec	*16*	
	Tues 24th	*10*	
	Fri 27th	*6*	
	Mon 30th	*10*	
	Tues 31st	*10*	*75 bottles*
	Wed 1st Jan	*4*	
	Thurs 2nd	*9*	
	Fri 3rd	*10*	

Important events were continually recorded on the log and observed in the school:

Jan 20th (Boys)	*H.M. THE KING died at 11.55 p.m.*
Jan 27th (Boys)	*Received notice that all W.R. Schools close tomorrow Jan 28th day of Funeral of his late Majesty King George V.*

The opportunities for academically inclined boys attending the Royston Secondary School are to be observed through the Log Books:

May 14th	*Received notice for Peter Briggs & Dennis Leach to attend Normanton Grammar School on 21st & 22nd May for Exam for transfer.*
July 31st	*Peter Briggs and Dennis Leach awarded CM Transfer Scholarships.*

The importance of the Mining Industry to the area can be seen:

June 8th	*Received notice that the school is to close on Monday June 22nd for Miners' Demonstration.*

On July 4th, the second school trip occurred, to Windsor, on which 60 boys took part. A more minor trip happened on July 21st:

> *I allowed IIIA to go on Nature Ramble to Notton.*

The importance of sport in the girls section is emphasised in the following entries:

July 6th	*1st Netball Team with Miss Littlewood took the 3.45 bus to Shafton to play a match.*
July 20th	*1st and 2nd Netball teams with Miss Littlewood and self took the 3.45 pm bus to Cudworth to play 2 matches.*

1936-37

The first teaching of Languages in the school is recorded on September 11:

> *French Class started with part of 1A Form (20). Miss Miller to try out an experimental class for two months.*

The girls' section was praised by Mr Griffiths, the local M.P.:

> *Examined registers and found correct. I was greatly impressed with the brightness of the Scholars. They all seemed to enjoy life.*

The tradition of Royston taking school trips continues with early consideration and forward planning:

Sept 30th (Boys)	*Staff Meeting Decided that School trip to Llandudno return via Liverpool by boat. Date June 19th.*
June 19th	*Annual Trip this Year to Llandudno by train & return via Liverpool to which steamer was taken to Llandudno.*
July 17th (Girls)	*School outing to Stratford on Avon to visit Shakespeare Memorial Theatre to see 'A Midsummer Night's Dream.' There were 50 in the party.*

The important place of sport and the local community in the life of the school, traditions still strong today, are shown:

Nov 13th	*Dr Pare presented a cricket bat to boy making best average in school matches. Presentation made at 3.00 pm by Dr Pare in the Hall. Dr Pare also promised another bat for next year.*

The problems inherent in a regional school were highlighted during November:

Nov 23rd	*Very dense fog & frost – visibility only 5yds – allowed Woolley children to leave 3.40 as buses had ceased running.*
Nov 27th	*Largely owing to the dense & persistent fog and sickness attendance is very bad this week Av 257 83.5%*

As well as weather, illness also proves to be recurrent factor in attendance:

Jan 18th	*Low attendance – Influenza and in afternoon rain & snow 187/282*

Jan 19th   *Received telephone message from Divisional Clerk to*
                  close at 4.00 pm till Feb 1st infuenza.

The stoicism and devotion to duty of teachers of the period can be
observed in the following entry:

Feb 15th   *H.T. out from 10.30 to 11.00 making arrangements for*
                  funeral of mother.

Another royal occasion:

March 6th   *Received notice of Coronation Holiday – 4 days viz.*
                  May 11.12.13.14
May 7th   *Mr W. Humphries of the D.S.C. made the presentation*
                  of the Souvenir Coronation spoons.

The Headmaster's continuing enthusiasm for taking boys for
gardening lessons is apparent throught the logs, the following being
an example:

April 22nd   *Took extra gardening as weather was fine.*
April 26th   *ditto*

1937–38

At the beginning of the school year, Mr Laycock received the HMI.
Report on his new school. The general findings were as follows:

Royston Senior Council School. No 953
Report by Mr S Taylor H.M.I.
Inspected on various dates in 1936 & 1937
Senior Boys
General – The school was opened in newly erected premises in August
1934. The present Head Master took charge from the school opening,
and has directed activities with energy and good sense. The team spirit
of the staff ensures a pleasant atmosphere of industry.

Schemes of work have been largely experimental and are receiving
the corrective reconsideration that is now essential.

The school is organised in four "Houses" for competition purposes.
Some contact is made with contributory schools, but it is evident that
certain points referred to the following subject reviews should be raised
in conference with the staffs of these schools.

The teachers are endeavouring to keep themselves well informed
concerning modern developments in special subject technique and aims.

It is observed that two boys 13-14 yrs are in form IC and seven
boys 14-15 are in IIC (one or two years behind their age).

The members of staff take a lively interest in the boys' games

Figure 7. A mid-1930s school football XI. Head Master, Mr G Laycock is on the left of the photograph. Several of the boys are wearing sporting medals. We also have a close view of the timber-clad building and the windows which had iron glazing bars. The area of glass, also used as roofing material for the corridors, was considerable. *Royston High School Archives*

Figure 8. The successful Royston Senior Boys' Cricket Team, winners of the Royston Schoolboys' Cup in 1937. The two bats, suitably displayed were much prized items. Several of the boys appear to be wearing Prefect badges. Despite their 'seniority' most of the lads are wearing short trousers. They are, standing (left to right): Mr G Laycock (Head Master), Fellows, Dale, Owen, Smart, Saxton, Downing and Mr R Southern. Seated (chairs) are: Jackman, Barker, Harrison (captain), Coatesworth, Greenfield and Mee. Seated (on the ground) are: Higginbottom and Coates (scorer?). *Royston High School Archives*

(Figures 7 & 8) *and some profit has been obtained from various school excursions. The sincerity with which the basic training of the initial period has been governed is, in itself, an assurance that the experience gained will be used to good effect in implementing future developments.*

All subjects were examined in detail and found to have many strengths, much as the recent OFSTED report of 2001. An example follows, taught, almost exclusively as it seems, by Gwilym Jones, the longest serving teacher, after the Headmaster, in school:

History – History is taught by a specialist teacher who exercises good influence over the scholars. He prepared the material of the lesson with the utmost conscientiousness and spares himself no pains in study and general thoughtfulness. Narrative is always interesting and the questions asked are searching. What is taught is thoroughly revised.

Yet, some improvement is possible in handling the subject or rather in selecting an adequate viewpoint. At the moment the teaching has to do too exclusively with what is sometimes called 'the dry bones' of History.

A more picturesque approach is needed. It is suggested that a time chart be constructed for continuous reference and historical material relating to the immediate environment of the school collected together. Again, certain groups of older scholars could be asked to undertake a little very simple research.

This would add life to the outline narrative of general History that the teacher is presenting.

In order to find time for these adventures, the present scheme may have to be remodelled.

Similar reports were received by Miss Parker:

<u>*Senior Girls'*</u>
<u>*General*</u>
Directed with vigour and competence by the Head Mistress, the spirit of the school is excellent, while the many and difficult problems of a critical period have been confronted with the necessary vision. Staff meetings are held regularly to ensure that teaching influences, syllabuses and organisation are readjusted as occasion and circumstances demand. The premises are clean, the girls maintain a neat appearance and the general implementing of the school life and activities suggests close supervision, and happy co-operation between the Head Mistress, the Staff, the scholars and the parents.

Much enterprise has been shown in endeavouring to solve the special problem of the 'C' stream. Further development of differentiation for the 'B' stream is necessary while here and there is a tendency to over teaching at the expense of individual endeavour.

School journeys, arranged for special and clearly defined purposes, are increasingly contributing to the reality of the teaching.

Individual records are kept, and it is interesting to note that they are not concerned only with subject attainment, but also with personal qualities and interests.

The school is doing well in Games, especially netball, while a hundred girls take a twelve week course of lessons in swimming.

The Head Mistress and her Staff deserve to be commended for their spirited and fruitful endeavour during this first three years of experiment. Good foundations have been laid and the outlook is most promising.

<u>Music</u>

Since the school opened, the Mistress specialising in Music has added very considerably to her own knowledge of the subject (Figure 9).

Efficient teaching is steadily raising the standards in Singing and Sight Reading and in general appreciation of Music. The Sight Reading books in use are over difficult.

Singing is tuneful, attack is precise and the results of careful training are evident in the phrasing and enunciation. There were cases in which the significance of the song could have been more fully realised by the groups. When the whole school sings simple well chosen songs or hymns the rendering is pleasing. Unison songs, descant and round are practised.

There have been years of uphill work and much credit is deserved for what has already been achieved. Recent entrants to the school are found to have received more early training in Music.

As yet this Department has no wireless set.

Figure 9. The Girls' School was noted for its drama performances. Here we can see a scene from a 1937 production in the new (shared) School Hall.
Brian Elliott Collection

Oct 14th   *Received notice the Thursday pm Oct 21st would*
            be half holiday to allow children to see the King and
            Queen on their S. Yorks tour.
            Football match Staff v School at 3.30.

On 25 November, Mr Laycock received a note informing him that
Carlton Spring Lane Council School would be transferring to the
Borough of Barnsley from the West Riding authority and that pupils of
secondary school age leaving the school would now attend Raley Senior
rather than Royston. Pupils already at Royston who lived in Carlton
would still have their travel costs met by the West Riding Authority, but
no children were to be admitted after 1 April 1938. This left Royston
with just two feeder schools: Midland Road and the Church School.

December of 1937 saw poor attendance due to bad weather:

Dec 4th   *Attendance low; bad weather.*
Dec 6th   "   " "   " *snowstorm.*
Dec 7th   *Attendance very low 226/275. Heavy snowfall.*
Dec 10th   *The attendance for the past 10 days or so has been*
            very low largely on account of the extremely bad
            weather.
Dec 23rd   *Closed for Christmas Holidays.*
            Past week has been worst for attendance that I have
            known, 79%.
Jan 21st   *Member of County Hall Staff called p.m. on*
            investigation of causes of bad attendance.

The convenience of having a railway station in Royston when organising
school trips can be seen in the arrangements for the 1938 outing:

Jan 9th   *Arrangements for School Trip*
            Date – June 25
            Leave Royston 6.30
            Arr. Windermere town 10.30
            Walk to Bowness
            Steamer to Ambleside about 12.00
            Lunch at Ambleside
            Steamer to Lakeside at 5.30
            Tea at Lakeside
            Leave Lakeside by train for Royston
            Fare 11/1d Adults 5/6d and a half Juniors
June 23rd   *Received particulars from Railway Co. of times of School*
            Trip on Sat.

I wonder if staff in those days had to go through all the administration and paperwork it takes to organise a school trip in the twenty-first century.

Although considerate of the health and well being of his pupils, Mr Laycock seems to have had short shift with people who crossed his path with regard to the organisation of health matters:

Jan 28th	*Mr. Parks, Sanitary Inspector called to see if immunisation for diptheria could be done in this dept as it was not convenient to H.T. for it to be done in Girls dept. As we have only 9 to do and there are 90 from other depts, suggested he try clinic.*
Feb 1st	*Miss Doris Peat gave lectures on teetotalism to IIC, IIA, IIA.*
June 28th	*School Nurse visited. As she came to school and went round without my knowledge I impressed on her that this must not occur again and that in future she must obtain my consent.*

Regular concerts were held in the schools:

April 6th (Girls)	*The School Concert. Items. 1. 'Brier Rose' A mime with music 2. 'The Fortune Ballot' - A Musical Play given to the Day School Children 5.30 pm 251 present.*
April 7th	*The above School Concert was given in the evening 7 pm to parents etc. The School Hall was full – Proceeds £14-8-5d.*

Mr Laycock's continued enthusiasm for gardening is seen throughout his entries:

May 31st	*Received about 10 tons stone for rockery.*

1938-39

The school year started in the Boys' Dept with a drop in the number on roll from 275 to 256 due to the absence of any boys from Carlton School, mentioned earlier.

An amusing incident is recorded on 20 September:

The following episode occurred today:-
A boy brought a note asking to leave at a quarter to 4
Teacher – "Why do you wish to leave early?"
Boy –   "Please sir I want to go to a party"
Teacher "Where?"
Boy   "At B_____'s; they have somebody dead!!"

More serious matters were brought into focus on 29 September when Mr Laycock recorded receipt of a circular regarding Air Raid Precautions, telling him that all West Riding Schools were to be closed if the government declared a state of emergency and asking him to forward names and addresses of all his staff should they need to be reassembled at short notice. Further action was taken on 21 November:

> *Received note from County Hall asking for 1 volunteer for ARP training to attend course at Barnsley Monday afternoons 2 to 4 for 5 weeks. Preference to be given to volunteer over 40 if any. Have arranged for Mr Jones aged 38 to go.*

The girls' school prepared for war:

Sept 28th   *A supply of gas masks fitted. Every girl and teacher present in the school has a gas mask.*

Sept 29th   *Remainder of the gas masks fitted. Every girl and teacher present in the school has a gas mask.*

An entry of 2 November (Boys) gives an indication of the length and organisation of the school day at the time and also the importance of collective worship and religion in the 1930s schools:

> *Registers marked. . . . . 8.55 - 9 a.m.*
>   "   *closed. . . . . 9.30 a.m. (Wed 9.40)*
>   "   *marked . . . . 1.25 - 1.30 p.m.*
>   "   *closed. . . . . 1.40 p.m.*
> *Religious Instr. . . . . 9 to 9. 30 a.m. (Wed 9.40)*
> *Secular Instr. . . . . 9.30 a.m. to 12 noon*
> *. . . . . 1.30 p.m. to 4 p.m.*
> *Recreation from. . . . . 11 a.m. to 11.10 a.m.*
> *. . . . . 3 p.m. to 3.10 p.m.*
> *Total time for Registration . . . 50 min*
> *Rel Instr. . . . . 160 min*
> *Rec. . . . . 100 min*
> *Sec Instr . . . . <u>1390 min</u>*
>   *1700*

A perennial problem in schools reared its head on 15 November:

> *Two boys, L____ S____ and H____ B____ turned in. It appears they have been playing truant for a fortnight and at the beginning of that period presented Drs notes. S____ had gone for them and B____ had not been seen by the Doctor.*

A tragic event occurred in December, 1938:

Dec 12th	*Mr Southern absent ill.*
Dec 13th	*Mr Southern absent. Typhoid suspected.*
Dec 14th	*It is with the deepest sorrow that I have to record the death of Mr Southern last night. He has been a loyal, devoted and conscientious colleague and was most enthusiastic in all he undertook. No man could wish for a better member of his staff.*
Dec 16th	*Funeral of Mr Southern takes place tomorrow at Brighouse 3.15 p.m. Staff have been asked to act as bearers.*

Ronald Southern had been a founder member of the staff at Royston Boys' School, teaching woodwork and organising teams and school excursions. He had received glowing reports throughout the records. His teaching career had lasted a mere 7 years and 8 months before his tragic death.

The fact that most children went home or into the village for lunch can be seen in an entry on 13 February 1939:

Enquiry re. Meal Arrangements.
Whether meals provided - no.

No of children taking midday meal for payment	0
No of certified undernourished chn	
(a) Receiving meals at Sch	0
(b) Receiving meals elsewhere	0
No of chn. who bring own food	20

An entry of 20 April gives the salaries of both teaching staff. Most teachers' salaries were around £240 pa, excepting Mr Jones who, due to his seniority, earned over £365 pa.

The remaining entries for the year show both school life carrying on much as normal in many respects but with indications of the difficulties which would have to be faced over the next six years:

May 8th (Boys)	*Children visited Palace* [cinema] *today at 4 p.m. to see film 'Tea growing in India'.*
May 10th (Boys)	*Received notice to say that officers of L.E.A. would visit to fix site of shelter trenches.*
	Did not arrive.
	Arrived 7 pm. Site selected.
June 17th (Girls)	*Saturday – School Outing to Liverpool and New Brighton. 86 girls and 8 teachers made up the party.*
June 19th (Girls)	*Caretaker reported 8 am that the school had been broken into during the weekend. Both storerooms - classroom stores – cupboards – drawers – desks broken into – contents rifled and much damage was done.*

June 20th (Girls)	*Dr. W.J. Melhuish, D.Sc., Ph.D., Analytical Chemist lectured to school this pm on:*
	1. Food, Rest and Growth showing the interaction of the three with due emphasis of need for earlier bed time.
	2. Tiny Plants a simple talk on bacteria emphasising importance of personal cleanliness and hygiene.
July 6th	*Police Sergeant called to ask boys to volunteer for messanger service A.R.P.*
July 19th	*Arthur Kirk IIIB sprained ankle on vaulting box.*
July 24th	*Mr Green and the boys left school at 3.52 to play cricket at Barnsley.*
July 28th	*Closed school for summer holidays, 4 weeks.*

By the time the school reassembled for the 1939-40 year, Britain was four days away from the Second World War.

1939-40

Aug 28th	*Returned to school all staff present.*
Aug 31st	*Examined all gas masks.*
	Received telephone call that school should not meet tomorrow but all staff to be on duty.
	School closed till further orders.

On 1 September 1939, Hitler ordered an attack on Poland. Britain carried out its threat to declare war on Germany. The Second World War had begun.

Sept 7th	*Circular 39/50 from Education Dept.*
	As regards the reopening of schools in Neutral Areas, it is recognised that it will be necessary for some provision to be made against the risk of attack from enemy aircraft, and as there may be some delay in providing the shelters which have been arranged for, it will not be possible to re-open schools in Neutral Areas for the present.
	I shall be glad to be informed when trench digging is commenced or when trenches have been completed ready for occupation at any school.
Sept 18th	*Re-opened school - No A.R.P. trenches ready.*
Sept 20th	*Miss Whitaker H.M.I. called re evacuated children at Notton.*
Sept 23rd	*Admitted one boy evacuee from Leeds.*
Sept 25th	*Received notice from Divl. Clerk that as this is not a*

	reception area, evacuees must be admitted.
Sept 26th	*Mr Burrough, H'craft Organiser called re. likely difficulty in obtaining supplies for timber and metal.*
Oct 6th	*The Garden has become overrun with weeds during holidays and A.R.P. closure. Have taken extra time to gardening to clear it.*
Nov 7th	*Mr Ward informs me he has obtained a post under the Air Munitions Meteorological Dept. He asks for his post to be kept open and for his release without notice.*
Jan 16th	*Have arranged with Miss Parker for Girls to have (in case of emergency) half the shelter (3 sections) until theirs is ready.*
Feb 2nd	*Gas masks examined and defective ones noted. This has been a shocking week for attendance - Average 145 74%. Heavy snow all week.*

This was the last entry in the school log by Mr Laycock. The following entries are by Mr Jones, Acting Head.

Feb 27th	*Air Raid Precaution drill taken 1.40pm. Time taken from sounding of alarm to last boy entering shelter - 2 mins, 50 secs.*
Mar 5th	*A.R.P. drill taken at 11.25 am All boys and staff had taken shelter in $2^1/_4$ mins, after sounding of alarm.*
Mar 20th	*Conducted further A.R.P. drill during playtime pm. Time taken for all to take shelter $2^1/_2$ minutes.*
Apr 10th	*A.R.P. drill taken at 2.50 pm while one class was in the hall doing P.T. Trials have now been conducted to acquaint boys of procedure under all conditions – ordinary class work, games, Phys Tr. and recreation.*
Apr 25th	*Received as a present from the Royal British Legion a pair of Stags Heads and Buffalo Horns.*
May 6th	***It is with very deep sorrow that I have to record the death of our Headmaster, who passed away on Friday 3rd May at 4 pm. Mr Laycock was a good master and a good friend to the boys and staff.***
May 7th	*The funeral of Mr Laycock took place today at Royston at 2 pm. Messers Davy, Green, Hanson and myself acted as bearers at the request of Mrs. Laycock. Boys lined up each side of the road opposite the school to pay their last respects to their departed Head.*

May 23rd	*Notified Divisional Clerk that Mr S Wood has been ordered to report for Military duties on Thur. 30th May.*
May 24th	*Conducted collection for Empire Day Overseas League Tobacco Fund for Soldiers, Sailors and Airmen. Result £1.14.0d.*
June 6th	*Notified the Divisional Clerk that Mr N M Taylor, metalwork master has been ordered to report for Military Service on Thursday 13th June.*
June 15th	*Invited parents to see Air Raid Shelters and to watch boys do their A.R.P. drill. More than 150 people attended and were very well satisfied with everything they saw.*
June 20th	*Attendance very low 54% am. due to Air Raid Warning given during night and lasting nearly 4 hours.*
June 25th	*Low attendance 61% due to A.R. warning during early hours.*
June 26th	*ditto 74% ditto*
July 5th	*In view of the fact that the Wood and Metalwork masters have left to join the forces it has been necessary to draw up an Emergency Time Table, dispensing with Wood and Metal for the time being.*
July 12th	*Received notice that school will remain open during August. Teachers will be given 2 weeks holiday in rotation.*
July 31st	*Sent four sacks of waste paper to Stores Dept.*
Aug 5th	*School opened today on a voluntary attendance basis. Teachers present were J.C.Crossland,A. Green and G.Hanson.*
Aug 9th	*The precentage of attendance was 10.5.*
Aug 16th	*I received notification this am from the Divisional Clerk that in view of the low attendance the School would close this pm. and re-open on Monday 2nd September on a full working basis.*

1940-41

The new school year began with Mr H Green taking up duty as Headmaster.

Sept 10th	*Messrs Hanson, Davy and Wilson ceased duty at this school today at 4 pm. They are proceeding to military service.*

Messrs Ward, Wood, Taylor, Hanson, Davy and Wilson were now serving in the armed forces. Mr Layclock was dead. Only two teachers who started the 1939-40 year were still in post, Mr A Green and Mr G Jones. This gives some indication of the disruption the war caused to a relatively small community like Royston. For the first time, women were appointed to teaching posts at Royston Boys'

School. Messrs Wilson, Wood, Hanson and Davy all returned to duty after the war, Mr Wilson serving until his retirement in 1972.

Sept 11th	*Mrs Webster and Mrs Townend took up temporary supply work here today am. Mrs Gorner took up temporary supply work here this afternoon at 1.30 pm.*
Oct 3rd	*Attended meeting at 3 pm. today to explore the possibilities of starting a school canteen to provide dinners.*
Oct 7th	*Rural Science Scheme inaugurated.*
Oct 28th	*The School Medical Inspector and Nurse called this morning on a nutrition survey. The names of 15 boys were proposed for free dinners.*
Nov 5th	*Mr R.F. Martin, Instructor in Horticulture to the Yorkshire Institute of Agriculture called re. the school garden.*

Mr Green was evidently a man of action, and his first year as head was spent in moving the school forward in a number of ways: academic achievement was addressed; extra-curricular activities were highlighted; attendance and punctuality became important issues for action; the first school magazine was produced, and the school received its first canteen and library (the latter in the current W1 room).

Dec 13th	*Staff meeting held today at which various aspects of school life were discussed. I asked for a widening of out of school activity, notably in the direction of hobbies and indoor recreational clubs.*
Jan 17th	*An oak shield in the woodwork shop was put up for competition for the first time this week. It is designed as a class trophy for meritorious attendance, and it is hoped to stimulate the boys into a greater zeal for punctual and regular attendance.*
Feb 17th	*Mr W Hamilton, Bee Expert, of the Yorkshire College of Agriculture gave a lantern lecture at 4 pm. today on Bees. About 90 boys attended. This lecture was run by the Bee Keepers Club as one of their activities.*
Feb 21st	*Today the half yearly examination was concluded. Subjects tested were:- English, Maths, Science, History, Geography, Art and Craft, Gardening (theory).*
Feb 24th	*Staff meeting to consider exam results and their bearing on a. Syllabus, b. Scope and type of teaching, c. Suitability of questions set, d. Type of Question Paper to*

	be employed in future examinations.
Mar 6th	*Canteen started here today.*
	Cook – Mrs Gibson. Helpers Misses Caswell and Sutton. 71 meals have been ordered for the boys dept on a basis of 4d [c2p] per meal per day.
Mar 13th	*Have been informed this morning that a room at this school is to be fitted out as a Library, and that information has to be forwarded to D.C. regarding surplus furniture thus rendered available.*
May 24th	*A conference was held at this school today between myself and the Heads of the contributory schools (Mr Thornton and Mr Cowan) with regard to the unification of method and syllabus in English, Arithmetic, Music and Geography.*
July 31st	*First 'Open Day' held today 2 to 4pm.*
	We had many parents up, although the day was bad, and they heard singing by the choir, and saw PT and Dramatics. Garden produce was on sale, and the first School Magazine ran through an edition of 400 copies.

The entries for the next three years are short on educational and organisational developments within the school and long on lists of staff change and absence. It was obviously a time of great problems for the school, a time of 'make do and mend' and keeping the school functioning in the trust of better times ahead.

Little mention is made of concerts, boys taking scholarships to Barnsley Technical School, or sports events which had been characteristic of the school up to this period. Whether this is an accurate reflection of school life during this period will only become apparent when more research has been completed. A small selection of entries follow, which reflect the lack of evidence and hints at some of the problems.

1941-42

Aug 31st	*School reopened this morning at 9 am. Mr Allsop has been called up for military service, and the vacancy caused has been filled by Mrs A Noble.*
Dec 1st	*From today the Juniors fed at this school canteen have withdrawn to the newly built JS Canteen. The National School from today will rec meals daily from this kitchen.*
March 17th	*Mrs Noble absent today with Chairman's permission - husband home on leave.*

1942-43

Aug 31st   *School opened this morning at 9 am. Caretakers cleaning has been adequately carried out, and those portions of the school not previously blacked out have now been done. All rooms can now be darkened.*

Sept 15th   *G.P.O. official called this morning re. the fixing of a telephoning in the school. It was decided for the sake of convenience to have the instrument fixed in Miss Parker's room.*

1943-44   *Annie Delia Berny took up service at this school today as clerical assistant. Age 15 date of b. 19th Oct 1928, Address – 116 Station Road, Royston.*

Jan 10th   *...the painting of the school has been completed... The question of the re-decoration of the hall after its mutilation by the Youth Movement has not yet been settled.*

1944-45

Aug 28th   *School reopened this morning at 9 am. Two absentees on the regular teaching staff, Mrs Townend and Mrs Webster. Mr Eric Garforth at present in training at St John's College York is appointed here for one week - no supply as yet for the other absence. The present position in regard to staffing is 3 men and 2 women to cover the work of the whole school.*

8/9th May   *The school was closed Tuesday and Wednesday for celebration of the Armistice...*

June 6th   *Mrs Holmes, WRDSC visited the school today... Comment was raised regarding the apparent low level of supplies of foodstuffs (in the canteen).*

These excerpts demonstrate the day to day pressures and rewards of running a small secondary school in the difficult days of the 1930s and 1940s.

Should any readers have memories of any of these personalities or events, I should be very pleased to hear from them. Their voices should be added to the wealth of information in the log books to form a truer picture of school life at the time. I can be contacted at Royston High School, Station Road, Royston, Barnsley, S71 4Q2.

10. JOHNNY WESTON'S MONK BRETTON: A SOCIAL CHRONICLE OF A VILLAGE IN THE FIRST HALF OF THE TWENTIETH CENTURY

by Barry Jackson

IN 1945 MY FATHER INTRODUCED me to what was to become one of the great joys of my life – cricket. When he took me to Wath to see one of the matches staged to celebrate the end of the war, and introduced me to the prodigious talents of Len Hutton and some of the visiting Australian Services Eleven, he could not have known how it would capture my imagination. A year later he moved the process a step further on when he introduced me to John Henry Weston (usually known as 'Johnny'). Johnny was Monk Bretton's sporting Pied Piper and I became yet another name on a long list of youngsters taken by him to see Yorkshire play at Bramall Lane, Headingley and Park Avenue. Each one received the same warning – 'tha welcome to come as long as tha behaves thisen'. My interest and good behaviour were rewarded over the next two years by numerous further invitations and culminated in my being put forward for Junior membership of the County in 1948. The trips were always by train from Cudworth Station (Johnny being at that time a 'ganger' on the railway, with an employee's concessionary travel pass) and as we went along he treated me to his own travel commentary, pointing out local landmarks and telling their story ('Tha sees that church. It's called Barnburgh, known as cat and man tahn, where t'cat killed t'man and t'man killed t'cat') was his watered down version of the death of Sir Percival Cresacre.

The Monk Bretton into which Johnny Weston was born in 1891 was definitely a village, as opposed to the mini town suburb of Barnsley (with a population of around 15,000) which it became when he died at the age of eighty-one. Late Victorian Monk Bretton was not even part of Barnsley, having its own urban district council whose jurisdiction went as far as Smithies and Old Mill, and being separated from the town which later absorbed it by its own green belt of agricultural land, worked by village farmers, of whom there were at least six. In common with so many villages of that time, it enjoyed a high degree of self-sufficiency. Its major employer of labour was the Monk Bretton Colliery, while its own transport station and the canal provided links with the rest of South Yorkshire. There were two

Figure 1. Monk Bretton National School in the early twentieth century. The teacher standing on the left is Frank O'Brien, who later moved with Mr Ward to Burton Road School.

schools – Lamb Lane Infants which Johnny attended in 1894 and the Junior School (Figure 1). The latter stood next to the vicarage and, after it closed in the 1930s, had a further life as Greenwood's toy factory (Green Monk Products) before it became Redfearn's Sports and Social Club. The Junior School was a church school thought to have been opened in 1846 by the National Society. Its last headmaster was Mr Fred Ward, the church organist, who had hoped to get the headship of the newly built Littleworth (now Priory) School, but was moved instead to Burton Road School for his last few years.

The village was served by several shops, the largest of which was the branch of the Barnsley British Co-operative Society. One of the small shopkeepers was Johnny Weston's father. In common with many residents of rural villages at that time the Westons kept a 'house shop', a small business run to supplement the father's income as a miner which later developed into a proper shop near the Cross and passed to his elder sister, Annie (Figure 2). It was this which brought young Weston into the activity in which he was to make his greatest contribution to village life – sport. Local tradesmen were allowed into the Cricket Club's Castle Ground to sell their wares to the spectators and young Johnny was expected by his father to join them by selling fruit, chocolate and stone bottles of ginger beer (at one old penny a pint) from a barrow. In 1903 the Cricket Club Committee decided that only members would be able to trade and so began a cricket club membership which lasted nearly seventy years and saw him successively as a player, committee man, groundsman (for thirty-four years) and honorary life member.

The young Weston was brought up as a Roman Catholic and at the age of ten went to the Catholic School in Barnsley. One of his proud boasts was that he carried the mitre for the Bishop of Leeds at the ceremony to lay the foundation stone for Holy Rood Church. He was encouraged to collect for the Catholic Church in his home village and this took him to the Klondyke area, a collection of terraced houses (including Faith, Hope & Charity Street) built around 1897 at the extreme edge of the village. These houses were obvious targets for his collecting as several of the early tenants were Catholic Irishmen.

Two important institutions in the village, which in their early years were very closely linked, were the Club (Monk Bretton Working Men's Club) and the Cricket Club. The Club had been formed around 1888 and was housed for its early years in farm buildings loaned for the purpose in Lievesley's farm until its present premises were built. The cricket club was formed shortly afterwards, occupying the field next to the farm which had always been used for recreational gatherings and was known as Gala Field. It was not the first cricket team in the village since a team from the colliery had for some years played in a field near the canal below the colliery. Johnny Weston always maintained that the cricket club was formed by members of the working men's club since, for a number of years, membership of the latter was a pre-requisite of membership of the

Figure 2. Annie Weston, Johnny's sister, outside her shop.

cricket club, and, on match days, beer was sold at the ground via the working men's club.

The Castle Ground, as it is now known, because of its proximity to 'Monk Bretton Castle' (the name given by locals to a folly built by the Wordsworth family, Figure 3), has always had a slope to it. This slope must have been even more pronounced before major work was done between 1898-99 in an attempt to make a more level field by removing soil from the top side (the pavilion side) and transferring it to the bottom side (the farm side). This was made easier by installing rails upon which pit tubs full of soil were pushed. These were no doubt supplied through the good offices of Mr Cheatter, the cricket club President. Joseph Cheatter was the Company Secretary at Monk Bretton Colliery. He had been a wicket keeper in his native Derbyshire in his younger days, but by the time of Johnny Weston's connections with the club, his movements were severely restricted by rheumatoid arthritis and he was brought to and from the ground in a pony and trap by the author's grandfather, who was the head horsekeeper, groom and coachman (ie, Mr Cheatter's chauffeur) at the colliery and had to carry his white-whiskered employer to his seat by the pavilion (Figure 4).

Figure 3. Monk Bretton Castle (late 1930s).

Figure 4. Harry Jackson (senior) holding the horse's head. The farrier, standing on the right is his son, Harry (junior).

The young Johnny Weston left school at the age of thirteen and went to work on the pit top as a pony driver. In 1906 he moved to Grimethorpe in the same capacity, but moved back to Monk Bretton Colliery nine or ten months later to work underground as a miner with his father. In 1904, after serving 'a cricketing apprenticeship', helping the groundsman Mr Riley by pulling the lawnmower and leading the horse (complete with leather boots to stop its hooves damaging the wicket) which pulled the heavy roller, Johnny played in

Figure 5. An early 'Monks v Cromwells' photograph.

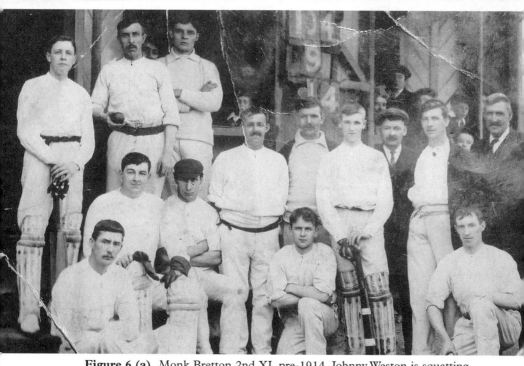

Figure 6 (a). Monk Bretton 2nd XI, pre-1914. Johnny Weston is squatting centre front.

the annual 'Monks v Cromwells' match for boys of the village (Figure 5). The 'Monks' came from the 'top end' (the village centre) and the 'Cromwells' from the 'bottom end' (the outlying parts of the village), forming two teams of indeterminate number, who afterwards sat

Figure 6 (b). Monk Bretton 2nd XI, pre-1914. Johnny Weston is standing, arms folded, wearing straw boater.

down to a tea specially provided for them. He must have shown some promise in the match, because, in the same year, he played his first match in the 2nd XI (Figures 6a & 6b).

The importance of Joseph Cheatter and the Colliery Company to the cricket club can be gauged from the fact that, when he died in 1912, the cricket club nearly closed down and had to be revived the following year. Cricket at the Castle Ground ceased during the First World War, the wicket square becoming a bowling green and the top side of the ground being turned into courts for a group of school teachers who formed a tennis club. During this time Johnny became involved in duties as a groundsman, a position which became official when the cricket club resumed in 1920.

From around 1921, Johnny's cricketing career blossomed. As he used to put it, 'It wasn't until I was thirty that I worked out what batting was all about'. He became a prolific run scorer for his home village and for two colliery sides (Rockingham and Monckton) when changes of job also dictated changes of cricket club. However, by the time that he was back at Monk Bretton and stopped playing cricket in 1945, he had left the mines and was working on the railway as a member of a track repairing gang. He was proud that, at one point in the 1920s, he was captain of the village cricket, football and snooker teams. At football he played pre-1914 for the Adult School team (Figure 7a) before switching in the 1920s to the Monk Bretton United XI (Figure 7b), which also included Herbert Manterfield, who was better known as the professional wrestler Bert Mansfield. Johnny was a tricky inside-forward who liked to keep close control of the ball. As he used to put it, 'I always had black and blue

Figure 7 (a). Monk Bretton Adult School Football XI, pre-1914. Johnny Weston is kneeling (arms folded), front row, second from the right.

Figure 7 (b). Monk Bretton United, early 1920s. Johnny Weston is seated on the ground, second right. The massive man seated in the centre is wrestler Herbert Manterfield. Next but one to him (with homburg hat and stick is Councillor J W Johnson, father of Syd Johnson[4]).

shins cos in them days owt above grass level got kicked'.

Monk Bretton in its village days had an abundance of characters. Doctor Hogg had one of the first cars seen there, but was such a slow and cautious driver that 'for a dare, some of the village lads lay down in the road in front of him!' When he spoke of characters, however, one name always came top of Johnny's list – 'Plonk' (pronounced by him as 'plunk') Jackson (no relative of the author). Joe Thomas Jackson acquired his nickname because of the names of his two sisters, Rosalina and Jestina and, to match these fancy names, the village lads renamed their three brothers 'Nebby', 'Shig' and 'Plonk'. 'Plonk' was always in trouble,

> he'd feight anybody and used to deliberately knock folks down at Pavilion skating rink in Barnsley to start a scrap. He did 'time' a time a two. During t'First World War he came home on leave swanking in a full officer's uniform. Where he got it from nobody knew, but after a day or two, t'police arrived to take him in. Once when I was on't way to t'Pavilion, I was stopped by a policeman at top of Regent Street and asked to form part of an identity parade at t'police station. When they brought t'suspect in it were Plonk and t'woman picked him out straight away. They paid us all a shilling and t'cheeky b.......r Plonk joined t'queue and tried to get a shilling!

As a child, Johnny went on trips to pantomimes at Leeds in waggonettes operated by Hobsons and Howarths, the same waggonettes for which he would earn one old penny a time by holding a horse outside the village pubs while the driver and passengers were inside drinking. As a young man, he regularly went to see the latest musical comedies in Barnsley at the Theatre Royal and Empire theatres. (The manager of the latter was Mr Smithson, whose daughter, Florence Smithson took the female lead in Lionel Monkton's *The Arcadians* during the original London run). To the end of his life, he would sing snatches of songs from such shows as *The Country Girl* and *The Geisha*.

The village had its own 'aristocracy' of wealthy, influential families who owned the large houses. The Addy family, who owned Carlton Main Colliery, lived at Osborne House, where they were followed by the Robinsons, and the Pepper family (owners of Monk Bretton Colliery) lived at Bank House, whose last owner in the 1960s, before it was demolished for residential development, was Dr Norris Pick. The Cliffe, which was eventually demolished to make way for Cliffe Court, was home first to the Marsden family (owners of what became the Star Paper Mill, where Asda now stands) and then to the family of auctioneers, the Lancasters. One of the village doctors, Dr McSweeney (who played in the cricket team) lived at The Ridings, which he sold to Mr Guest the Barnsley grocer when he himself moved to Bank House ('McSweeney once pulled me a tooth aht in't passage at his house, then gave me a tanner and told me to go home and be a good lad'). In the 1920s and 1930s, Mayfield (Figure 8) on Thoresby Avenue was home first to Barnsley's Town Clerk, Mr Mason and then to the White family of Ashwin-Whites Solicitors, before being bought in 1937 by the author's Uncle, Barnsley tobacconist, George Bell. After his and his wife's death in 1966, the house was demolished and the two and a quarter acre site used to build the Mayfield estate.

Figure 8. Aerial view of Mayfield, *c.*1950.

Figure 9. Monk Bretton church procession (late 1920s) with Monk Bretton Brass Band.

One place with which another form of village 'aristocracy' was associated was the Monk Bretton Club. This was somewhat different from what is now thought of as a working men's club. It had a definite educational and improving aim to it, part of the premises being used as a reading room and library, while room was provided for rehearsals by a village band and village orchestra. Standards of dress were maintained and, pre-1912, Johnny was reprimanded for going to the club minus collar and tie and wearing his clogs. This lapse did not, however, count against him in the long term and, in 1923, he was elected to the committee, joining such village worthies as J W Johnson, William Carr, J W Shaw (all Councillors on Monk Bretton UDC) and Joe Dodd. The latter was a local shopkeeper, an extreme socialist and self-proclaimed atheist, who showed himself in the view of many villagers to be the best Christian in Monk Bretton by the way that, through his shop, he cared for the village's striking miners during the 1926 strike. During the same dispute the club cared for members with issues of free fish, while the cricket ground provided the venue for interminable cricket matches to fill in the time between sessions of 'coal-picking'. As if to destroy the idea that the club was too sedate and well-behaved, Johnny recalled that one member gave vent to his frustration in the reading room by casually setting fire to the copy of the *Daily Sketch* being read by a fellow member who had refused all morning to surrender it!

The club was not the only drinking place in the village. Monk Bretton had the *Pheasant* (Figure 11), the *Norman Inn*, the *Sun Inn*, the *Bridge*

Figure 10. Croft House (pre-1912). The canal bridge can be seen on the right.

Figure 11. The *Pheasant Inn* in the time of Wilfred Harrison.

Inn and the *Butchers Arms*; and the men of the village made full use of these hostelries. Some of the most notorious drinkers came from the colliery-owned houses at Day's Croft, an area which probably took its name from an old bleach croft. This settlement was made up of three rows of houses (later, after World War Two, to be demolished and buried under the colliery spoil heap) and Croft House, a large three-storey house divided down the middle, with Joseph Cheatter (the Company Secretary) occupying the front part, and the author's grandfather, Harry Jackson and his family having the back part and garden. The whole area was near the canal and was reached by a lane which came out by the *Sun Inn*, which therefore, became the Day's Crofters' pub. The *Sun Inn* was kept by Wilfred Harrison, whose niece, Madge, came to live with him when her parents died. He later moved to the *Pheasant* where Madge met and married the young Johnny Weston (as Johnny put it, 'she only came for a fortnight and she never left').

In matters of religion, the village of Monk Bretton had a long history right back to the building of Monk Bretton Priory.[1] Although this made the village an important religious centre, it did not have a church of its own, being part of the parish of Royston until 1838 when a new church was built. The building must have been an unsatisfactory one and in 1876 the foundation stone was laid for the present St Paul's which was officially opened by the Archbishop of York on 6 May 1878, the old church having been demolished. Although born and brought up a Roman Catholic, Johnny regarded the Anglican St Pauls as his village church, and demanded that this was where his funeral should take place. The village had, however, other claims to religious fame. 'Burton' as it was then known, was a noted seventeenth and eighteenth century centre for Quaker meetings and retained its Quaker burial ground until the mid-twentieth century.[2] A nineteenth century Wesleyan Reform chapel developed a leaking roof and had to be pulled down around 1950, it congregation moving to nearby Ebenezer premises until a new building was erected and opened in 1963.

The dominant figure in religious affairs in Johnny Weston's day was Father Mercer (as he was known) who was the vicar of St Paul's from 1918-39 (when he moved to St Wilfrid's, in Cantley, near Doncaster where he remained until his death in the 1950s). The Reverend John Alban Ernest Mercer (Figures 9-12) was a graduate of Durham University and had been a teacher in the East End of London before training for the priesthood. His educational experience served him well in the pulpit, and his reputation as a preacher earned him a wide following in the Barnsley Deanery and brought full church attendances. He was an excellent pianist who

Figure 12. The Reverend John Mercer accepts a gift from babe-in-arms Barry Jackson at St Paul's Gift Day, December 1935.

took groups of parishioners to musical productions and always had them to the vicarage beforehand to explain operatic themes and plots etc. He was a bachelor 'wedded to the church' and his only family responsibility was to his unmarried sister who kept house for him. He became a true shepherd of his flock, looking after all aspects of the welfare of his parishioners. If it was noticed that he had a new suit, someone was at the vicarage door post haste to acquire the old

Figure 13. Monk Bretton St Paul's Football XI, 1918. The photograph (by Lamb & Co) is taken at the side of the vicarage.

Figure 14. The 'Harvest Queen', 1937. Back row (L-R): Margaret Crossland, Beryl Skilton, Jean Buttery, Sheila Coles, Bessie Howarth, Audrey Wray, Molly Thompson, Joan Lisle, Murial Maw, Marjorie Birkinshaw. Front row (L-R): Jean Barton, Barry Jackson, Donald Harston.

one. His churchmanship was Anglo-Catholic, and he had close links with and the support of the Halifax family of Hickleton Hall. He encouraged membership of the church by the development of a full range of social activities. During his early months, he began a St Paul's football club (Figure 13) of which the author's father was one of the first members, while dramatic productions such as 'East Lynne' and an annual pantomime were staged in the Church Hall. A trip to Oberammergau led him to stage Monk Bretton's own 'Passion Play' in 1938 and a thriving Sunday School was built up. The latter had three important pieces of pageantry each year – the crowning of the May, Rose and Harvest Queens (Figure 14), each with appropriate dialogue and Christian symbolism. After John Mercer's departure,

with the advent of World War Two, a new patriotic dimension came with the adding of a soldier, sailor and airman to the Rose Queen festivities and the author has vivid recollections of being in RAF uniform, delivering John of Gaunt's speech from Richard II about 'this sceptred Isle, this Royal throne of Kings etc' on the lawn of the Lancaster family home 'The Cliffe' which was also the venue for the church garden parties (Figure 15). In 1935, the old monastic links were revived when John Mercer

Figure 15. Patriotism at the 'Rose Queen' ceremony c.1943. Soldier (Norman Saunders), Airman (Barry Jackson), Sailor (Trevor Moxon).

Figure 16. Open-air service at Monk Bretton Priory, late 1950s.

obtained permission from the Ministry of Works to hold an open-air service in the ruins of Monk Bretton Priory, preceded by a pageant tracing the building's history (Figure 16). The service developed into an annual event, the singing being accompanied by Ernest Exley (the church organist), playing the accordion. The service lapsed in recent years, but an attempt was made last year to revive it.

The years of Father Mercer have always been regarded as a golden age at St Pauls, but there was always one incident which formed a blot on the record as far as the author's father (who was at that time a member of the Parochial Church Council and a former altar server) was concerned and this was the dismissal around 1929-30 of the village headmaster from his post as church organist and choirmaster. Frederick Ward was a sociable man who liked a drink and, on the Christmas Eve in question, he was in a happy mood and at the midnight service played very loudly. (He did not, as rumours circulating afterwards maintained, play 'Yes we have no bananas'; a fact confirmed for the author by ninety-year-old ex-choir member Sid Richardson shortly before he went to live with his daughter in Canada[3]). Instead of quietly asking his son Denis Ward to take over, John Mercer publicly stopped the service and said that it would only continue 'when the organist has left the organ stool and the church'. The outcome was that a thriving choir broke up, most of the choir men following their choirmaster.

Shortly afterwards the Church was refurbished (Figure 18) and the organ removed from the front of the church to make way for the new Lady Chapel. It was the end of a robed choir at the front of the church and by the time, in May 1932, that a new organ presented by

Figure 17. Ernest Exley at the keyboard of the Ritz cinema's Wurlitzer organ.

the Lancaster family was dedicated in a choir gallery at the rear of the church, the Parish had a new organist, Ernest Exley, who held the position for thirty-one years. Ernest, who also became the licensee of the *Norman Inn*, was a prominent Barnsley musician who had been a pianist in the days of the silent films at the Empire and the Alhambra in Barnsley and later deputised at the Ritz cinema organ (Figure 17). He played with the Mayfair Dance Orchestra and at the church ran all the shows and pantomimes, in which he always played a dame. His musical skills also shaped his war service in the RAF where he was stationed at Blackpool, becoming music librarian to Sidney Torch who ran the RAF Concert Orchestra. Ernest used to joke that he was awarded the BEM (Blackpool Edurance Medal!).

As part of the church refurbishment two pieces of furniture were acquired from an artist/sculpture whom John Mercer had come to know during his teaching in London's East End. Charles Wheeler carved the Rood (the figure of Christ in glory on the cross hanging over the sanctuary) and the Stations of the Cross which decorate the walls. In later years, the artist became Sir Charles Wheeler, President of the Royal Academy.

In his later years, when cricketing was done, Johnny Weston settled down easily into the role of village sage and character (Figure 19). He would be seen in the cricket field most summer evenings; a stocky red-faced man dressed in old overalls and sporting a battered panama hat as he worked on his beloved wicket. He bemoaned the acquisition of a lighter motorised roller (Figure 20) from Northamptonshire County

Figure 18. The refurbished St Paul's Church, Monk Bretton, with Charles Wheeler's Christ in Glory on the Cross hanging from the Sanctuary arch.

Cricket Club, preferring to press gang players on practice nights into a team to drag the heavy roller which he had pulled as a boy. His winter message to the committee was always the same: 'Give me ten pahnd of seed and ten pahnds worth of water and I'll get you a reight wicket'. He was especially hard on young batsmen who got caught behind early in their innings whilst trying to cut or pull (the shots which he, as a little man, played so well):

> *Tha doesn't cut so early in thi innings. T'basis of t'game should be sound defence. Tha can't mek runs when tha back in't pavilion.*

As the light faded on practice nights, he became the focus for a group of players; the story-teller and his audience. Then the fun and the yarns started...

> *Old Bill Senior dahn at Carlton hed legs as thick as blood veins. He once went in to bat wearing just one pad and t'ball hit t'other leg and broke it...We hed a player who were a nice chap but he had a terrible*

Figure 19. Monk Bretton 2nd XI (1963 or 1964). Johnny Weston is standing on the left and the author is the captain, seated, wearing a cap.

squint. He took his guard at Felkirk and waited – and waited – and waited until, after a minute or two, t'umpire said 'When tha ready we'll start.' He thought he were looking at point! ...I once played in a football match which we drew yet none of the opposition turned up. There were a local rule which said that to claim t'points you had to walk t'ball into the opposing goal. We started messing abaht doing fancy passing until one silly b....r let it run over t'side line. T'ref said right it's a throw in to t'others and there's nobody to take it so you've drawn.

Figure 20. After the presentation of the new motor roller to Syd Johnson (joint groundsman with Johnny Weston), ladies of the Cricket Supporters Club who had helped raise the money, pose for a photograph with Syd. Left to right, they are Beatrice Moxon (grandmother of Yorkshire & England cricketer Martyn Moxon), Edith Livesey, Dorothy Freeman, Dorothy Beckley and Doris Jackson. Beatrice was the cook for Lancasters at the Cliffe and her husband, Percy, was the gardener.

By the time of his death in 1972, Johnny Weston's village of Monk Bretton had virtually gone (Figure 21). Employment patterns had changed, most of the farms had disappeared and so had the colliery. Other firms had come and gone; a chemical company which had given its name to part of the village (Distillery) closed, the tank factory built in wartime to provide tanks for the British Army had been taken over by Frasers who had switched to the production of tanks for storage. From 1945 to the early 1970s Redfearn National Glass acquired land at Distillery and Klondyke, gradually switching its production from its works at Harborough Hills, Barnsley, and in the process swallowing up Frasers, the old canal and part of the now defunct railway link from Barnsley to Cudworth. Large housing estates built on land once farmed by the Lievesleys, the Roberts, the Richmonds, the Wilkinsons and the Chattertons swelled the village population to seven times what it had been at the start of the twentieth century. Then, in the 1950s, the planners of the Barnsley Council committed what such as Johnny Weston regarded as the ultimate act of vandalism. In a desire to build a post-war 'New Jerusalem', they started upon a programme of council house building,

Figure 21 (a-e). A selection of old buildings of Monk Bretton painted in the early 1950s by Reg Gosling. These paintings were bought for Redfearns by Dr Stanley Race and photographed there by Philip Hartley.

(a) The Garrison Houses   **(b)** Top of Littleworth Lane
(c) High Street with the old Wesleyan chapel.   **(d)** Eli Roberts' Butchers Shop

(e) The old *Norman Inn*

but this was before the planners were conservation-minded. Instead of retaining the old properties in the centre of the village which were so full of character and modernising their interiors, they demolished them and shipped the inhabitants off to other council estates in Barnsley such as Athersley and Kendray. The heart was torn out of the village and most of the people so uprooted never returned. By the time that Johnny Weston died, the village in which he had grown up, loved and served had also died and been replaced by what he saw as an alien landscape.

Notes and References

1. Details of the foundation of Monk Bretton Priory etc, from Rowland Jackson's *History of Barnsley*, published in 1858.
2. Details of the Quakers in Monk Bretton may be found in Brian Elliott's *The Making of Barnsley*, published by Wharncliffe Books in 1988.
3. Sidney Richardson was the son of Alderman Thomas Richardson, who was the Mayor of Barnsley during World War Two. Sid played cricket at Monk Bretton during the 1930s and went for a few seasons with Johnny Weston and Syd Johnson to play at Monckton, before returning to Monk Bretton CC post-1945. A local government officer, he was in charge of Barnsley Council's Housing Department when he retired. A lifelong churchman, he sang in Monk Bretton Church choir and later with the Barnsley Musical Society Chorus. Latterly, he was, for a number of years, Churchwarden of St Edwards Church, Barnsley. His eyesight was not so good when he left Barnsley in 2000, and the author gave him copies of the Johnny Weston tapes to take to Canada with him.
4. Sydney Stuart Johnson (1898-1988), usually known as 'Syd', was something of a cricketing legend in South Yorkshire (chiefly with Monk Bretton, but with short spells before at Barnsley and Monckton). His slow left arm bowling brought him between 1913 and 1968 an estimated 10,000 wickets, including all ten wickets on three occasions. At the age of sixty-five he robbed himself of a fourth 'all ten' by taking a slip catch and finishing with 9 for 74. In early September 1968, having announced his intention to retire because of an old football injury, he played for Monk Bretton's Second XI in the Council Minor League under the author's captaincy. He declined the chance to open the bowling and add to his tally of wickets because 'it would not be fair'. He fielded and then bowed out of competitive cricket without fuss. He was a cricketing gentleman who also served as club treasurer and coach, and served in tandem with Johnny Weston as groundsman.

The main source of this article are three hours of taped interviews with Johnny Weston made by the author in the 1960s. All illustrations are provided from the author's own collection.

11. CANON SORBY AND SOME CHARACTERS OF OLD DARFIELD

by Margaret Mann

Introduction by Brian Elliott

Several years ago I received an excellent manuscript from Margaret Mann based on her research and memories of people, places and events relating to the village and parish of Darfield (Figure 1). It was clear to me that her extensive writings would not only appeal to anyone with personal or family connections in the area but also have much wider interest. Unfortunately, it wasn't possible to incorporate all of her work in a single *Aspects* volume. However, I was very pleased to facilitate an edited version, for *Aspects of Barnsley 6,* based around her own childhood memories and family history, under the title 'Memories of a Darfield Childhood'. Margaret's sensitive and literary style captures a period of English rural life that has long

Figure 1. A multi-view picture postcard of Darfield, posted in Darfield in 1914. *Margaret Mann*

disappeared, without being over-romantic or too nostalgic about the 'good old days'. Apart from her accounts of her own family we are provided with a more than useful insight into the significant role that farming still occupied in Darfield as it did in most Barnsley areas during the 1920s and 1930s. In her first essay we are treated to cameos of several Darfield characters: Joe Gamwell and 'Juddy' Green (in relation to the old *Cross Keys* and *Ring O'Bells* respectively); and of course the Taylors of Middlewood Hall. There were others too, including local doctor Will Castle, and shopkeepers and craftsmen such as clockmaker Joe Gartrey, cobbler Tim Marshall, and Veniah Bailey, who operated a 'tiny greengrocery'. What follows is another edited extract from her writings, featuring Canon Sorby, Darfield Rectory and a few local characters. Margaret also acknowledges the anecdotes passed on to her by her mother and the late Alec Clarney who, in his own lifetime, did so much to support, campaign and promote the village of Darfield and its neighbourhood.

Canon A E Sorby, Rector of Darfield

IN 1892, CANON ALFRED ERNEST SORBY (Figure 2) was appointed Rector of Darfield, in succession to Reverend Folliart Henry Pannant Cook. Canon Sorby held the living until his death some forty-two years later.

Brought up in the traditions of a country gentleman, Canon Sorby had his finger on the pulse of rural life, and his parishioners recognised their good fortune in having such a dedicated man as their Rector. Although well-liked, he could also be extremely frank and possessed a strong individuality, qualities which commanded both admiration and respect, even during disagreements.

A tall, erect man, he was a model of strong, upright Christianity and a shining example for the Anglican ministry. That a man of his considerable ability was content to remain in a depressed mining parish, when undoubtedly he could have moved on to work in wider pastoral fields, was a fitting tribute to his limitless devotion and courage. 'Benign he was,

Figure 2. Canon Sorby in middle age. *Margaret Mann*

and wondrous diligent; and in adversity full patient', was a fitting text quoted by the Bishop of Sheffield at his well-attended funeral.

Among his clerical associates, Canon Sorby was recognised as a man of great worth, whose effects and influence were always on the side of preserving dignity and sanctity in church government. He was, in a way, a very mild man, and yet so strong and tenacious when ecclesiastical rights were challenged. His views were often sought on difficult problems affecting both the spiritual life and administration of parish, diocese and province; and no one appreciated his loyalty and sound judgement more highly than his Bishop, who, there is reason to believe, frequently had recourse to him as a counsellor and confident.

Canon Sorby had qualities and abilities that marked him out as a scholar but he never lost the 'common touch', or became so preoccupied with 'great things' as to lose concern for his parishioners. He had a kindly word for everyone. He was a perfect gentleman, having high regard for the courtesies of life, and was a good host. Darfield Rectory entertained many notables, including Lady Haigh (widow of Field Marshall Haigh), and Lord Harewood who came to Darfield to open the British Legion Club.

He had an artistic mind, loved beautiful things such as flowers and pictures, and was passionately fond of children. Young people so difficult to retain for church work, rallied round him of their own accord; and one of the most successful features of his work was his Young People's Bible Class (Figure 3).

Figure 3. This photograph, showing an adult Bible Class, was taken at Middlewood Hall in *c.*1926. Canon Sorby is the unmistakable figure at the centre of the large group.

Canon Sorby was a fighter with a profound respect for, and no mean knowledge of the law, and was always ready to avail himself of the ammunition the constitution allowed him. This side of his character was revealed shortly after he came to Darfield. The West Riding Education Authority took legal proceedings against a number of his parishioners for withdrawing their children from school to attend religious service in the parish church on Ascension Day; and though he attended court to defend them, the decision of the Justices was in favour of prosecution. The Canon was not prepared to accept defeat. He appealed to the King's Bench, where, as a result of action, he won for parents throughout the country, the charter of religious liberty embodied in the celebrated judgement which became known as The Ascension Day Case. After that he took up many other causes, and was always treated with respect where legal matters were concerned.

It was under Canon Sorby's ministry that a considerable amount of restoration work took place to All Saints' church (Figure 4). The

Figure 4. All Saints' Church during the incumbency of Canon Sorby. *Margaret Mann*

first phase was the removal of plaster from the walls of the sanctuary. The original workmanship and artistry of medieval stonemasons was revealed for the first time in many generations.

Sorby was also a keen sportsman, and had an inherent fondness to travel and the open-air life. Moreover, he had the gift of communicating impressions of his experiences to others. There may be some who remember with great pleasure, stories of his egg-collecting expeditions; his journeys to the Faeroes, his voyages with the trawlermen to the northern fishing grounds, and of his visit to India where he spent two or three absorbing months with his children, travelling and sight-seeing. It was typical of his indomitable spirit that at the age of seventy-three he was ready and willing to undertake such an arduous journey in the hope of regaining strength. Though immaculate in bearing and manners, he was always prepared to 'rough-it'; and in fact thoroughly enjoyed the unconventional experience. On his trips to the Faeroes, he associated freely with lonely fisherfolk, and developed an expert knowledge on the subject of whaling. He could speak with some authority on the people and customs of northern lands.

Canon Sorby's tenure as Rector of Darfield was notable for his consolidation in 1906, of the first and second mediety; thus ending the divisions due to a divided priesthood which had existed from Anglo-Saxon times, between a rector and a vicar. Canon Sorby is buried in Darfield churchyard near the west door of the church he loved and served for half a century.

Lizzie Jobling, the Sorby's House Maid

Lizzie Jobling was a live-in maid, sleeping in a cold attic bedroom with one day off a month, and Sunday afternoons when she did her courting. Lizzie worked in Darfield Rectory (Figure 5) from leaving school at fourteen until she married, eleven years later.

> *It was hard work in those days,* she reflected when talking to me, *and our wages were only six shillings* [30p] *a week and our keep; But we had some jolly times!* said Lizzie, her eyes twinkling.

> *We were up at half past six in the morning, and I had to get the huge fire going in the kitchen, clean the stove, its four ovens, and all the flues, with nothing but a hard brush and dustpan. There was some beautiful old furniture; and I remember the huge rocking horse in the nursery – we maids were having fun upstairs in the children's nursery*

Figure 5. Darfield Rectory in Edwardian times. *Brian Elliott*

one day; one maid was underneath the great rocking horse's belly, pushing it, and I was riding it – when in walked the Canon!

There was a vast hallway for us to clean – and no sweeper. It had a full-sized billiard-table and large display cases of birds' eggs collected on the Canon's holidays, as far away as the Orkneys; and we dusted and polished the black oak Elizabethan dresser, and all the Canon's old polo sticks. The winters were bitterly cold in those days; we put down dozens of eggs in water-glass in the larder, and we could bounce them, they'd frozen so hard. The flagged floors were sparsely covered with mats and there was a dark, back-stairway and landing; and we maids had to sweep all those bare stone stairs. We filled stone hot-water bottles with boiling-water and put them in the feather beds. Everyone had their own candlestick that was kept on the hall table to light us up the draughty stairs, and to our remote attic corners. There was gas lighting only in the downstairs rooms, so that the last person to bed had to turn out the gas – not a pleasant duty when the place was over-run with mice that squeaked and scurried on the stone stairs as your candle-light caught their eyes in the darkness!

In those days, Lizzie continued, *Boys raised their hat to the squire, the doctor and the parson. I remember Canon Sorby telling us maids that we must never go out without wearing a bonnet.*

I can remember Watson's School at the top end of the churchyard; it was shaded by huge horse-chestnut trees, where boys in little Norfolk jackets with lace collars, scrambled for conkers: Mr and Mrs Revel lived at the Rectory Cottage. 'Revel' was gardener cum odd-job-man at the rectory, and his wife was cook there; they had a cairn terrier called Nettle – aptly named. The Canon's wife bred cairns, and she called her own dog Darkie. It used to sit perkily on the settee, and we daren't move it off!

I always seemed to get caught out if I did anything I shouldn't, said Lizzie, wryly. *Like the time I got the laundry-maid drunk on rhubarb wine, then had to tackle all the washing myself, all the household linen, all the maid's caps and aprons! Once I tried to knock down some pears in the rectory orchard but Canon Sorby soon discovered my misdoings. We could never play truant from church on a Sunday morning without being found out. Cook always asked us to recite the Canon's text from his sermon; but I remember the day there was a fire at the rectory, and it burnt all the Rules and Regulations – we called it a fire of convenience!*

The village was really lovely in those days. As I walked to the rectory everyone knew everyone else, it was such a close-knit community. The family Bible was kept in the cottages of most folk instead of the clock! There was Veniah Bailey's greengrocery shop, then Boiling's fish shop, both under thatch; Dr Will Castle at Thornhill, the big house beyond the old copper beech; then there was Field House at the corner of Mary Lane where my grandma Jobling lived; and an old sailor who played the mandolin. George Dickinson fetched the milk right from Crook House farm every morning. He drove his horse and milk float round all the by-lanes and footpaths to keep the paths in public use but he was a cantankerous old chap. I remember being carried as a child in a winter thick with snow, but George Dickinson still managed to get round with the milk, pulling steadily on the horse's rein and calling softly to encourage it, 'Whey there: whoa there!'

We had lovely parties in the Rectory. I remember one such occasion when all the fine ladies of the neighbourhood arrived, donned up in their fancy frills and furbelows, when in walked Miss Phyllis Taylor, the squire's daughter, in a dove-grey velvet gown, just as plain as the others were fancy. It was a lovely soft velvet that you could crush in your hand and not crease, its only adornment being one diamond brooch – yet she looked lovelier than all the fussily-dressed women.

'Taffy' the Shepherd

'Taffy', a Welshman, was the shepherd at Barker's farm, Edderthorpe. He lived in a dirty old hut on wheels located in the middle of a field, and surrounded by his flock of sheep. A small, spare man, his no-date hat and clothes were swarthy with constant contact with the sheep, seven days a week, and smelt strongly of their oily fleeces. Lambing was a very busy time for him, tending the ewes day and night. You could see him trudging round the field looking for ewes about to lamb. It was a lonely life, but he loved the work and sang hymns to himself in a light, cracked voice, to relieve the quietness.

Mounted on an old rusty bike, his weekly shopping routine in the village was to call at the Co-op for his meagre fare of bread, tea and sugar etc, then a visit next door to the butchers where he cadged a bone for Meg, his black and white sheep-dog. From the chemist he collected his bottle of cough mixture, and finally he dropped by at the *Cross Keys* for liquid refreshment. For an hour or two, he chatted with the locals, then at three o'clock, turning out time, he would unsteadily mount his bike, and wobble up Church Street and along School Street. There was little traffic to hinder his erratic progress. He had to concentrate hard at peddling along Saltersbrook Road and back up the incline towards Edderthorpe; but when he reached the crest of the hill overlooking the farm, a transformation took place. Taffy lifted his feet off the pedals, let go the handlebars, and with an exultant cry he would free-wheel at manic speed downhill, until he crash-landed at the farm.

Taffy minded his sheep for many more years until one day his faithful collie, Meg, was found howling outside his hut where he was found dead, lying on a bunk of rags. Joe Gamwell, landlord of the *Cross Keys*, had a collection to help with funeral expenses for the old man who had worked day and night to tend the sheep he loved.

Kate Bush, herb beer, wine and syrup brewer

She was a strange-looking figure, with the swarthy face of an old peasant woman, and something in her appearance of bats wings or old cobwebs. Indoors, she wore a mop-cap, and when she sallied outdoors she wore a battered felt hat with a drooping brim that hid the old woman's withered features. She was 'of the fields' and had great knowledge of herbs and their uses; comfrey and dolphin were always to hand for anyone suffering from aches and pains. Her fusions and potions were available for a few coppers.

Kate brewed and sold herb beer, but her greatest skill was making elderflower wine and syrup. The latter was a rich, dark syrup, and mixed with a little hot water in winter, a good dose warmed your chest and warded off coughs and colds.

During the early summer you could see her walking the lanes collecting elderflowers; and in autumn, clad in an old black coat and a shadowy brimmed hat, armed with a crook-handled stick, and carrying a large rush-basket, she went out collecting elderberries. When she had brewed the potent syrup and poured the rich wine-coloured mixture into bottles, she made it available to her grateful customers at a shilling a time.

'Rhubarb' Dick

Dick Henderson lived in a tiny red-brick cottage alongside Bullins Dyke, midway between between Low Valley and Wombwell. Dick grew rhubarb on a large scale in the 1920s, hence his nickname, 'Rhubarb Dick'. There were fields full of rhubarb alongside the lane to Cuckstool Terrace and Fattycake Row. (The name from lardicakes thrown onto the shelves of old Yorkshire ovens.) Here the land was flat and fertile, enriched by manure and straw that Dick threw out of the sheds where he stabled his old nag that carted the piled boxes of rhubarb to the local station, and then to Wombwell market. His trousers, fastened below the knee with a piece of string, his hobnailed boots weighed half a stone, and a felt hat gone basin-shaped, comprised his rig-out. His rhubarb was in low, dark sheds in his fields, row upon row of crowns. Dick carefully cultivated their early growth so that he could get a good price when he sent the pink and slender sticks to market.

When Rhubarb Dick died, no one was interested in growing rhubarb any longer; and so his long sheds were demolished, the crowns uprooted, and his fields turned into a greyhound track.

Charles Howard Taylor's funeral

When the squire of Middlewood Hall (Figure 6) died the heart of the village was touched. From the Hall to the Church, the coffin was drawn on a farm waggon, to which was yoked a magnificent chestnut horse from the estate. Immediately preceding this was another farm waggon on which a profusion of wreaths and floral tributes were heaped. Other conveyances were dispensed with, the whole band of mourners walking from Middlewood to the church. Upon the coffin was a huge cross of red roses, from the family.

Country funerals were picturesquely impressive celebrations of life, steeped in custom. The stroke of death makes a wider space in the village circle, and is an awesome event in the tranquil uniformity of rural life. The passing bell tolls its knell in every ear; it steals with its pervading melancholy over hill and vale, and saddens all the landscape.

Figure 6. Charles Howard Taylor c.1860-1935. *Darfield Museum*

12. CHARLES WARD, MASTER AT DARTON'S VICTORIAN GRAMMAR SCHOOL

by John Goodchild M Univ

IN THE WRITER'S LOCAL HISTORY Study Centre at Wakefield is a colourful illuminated address (Figure 1) presented to Charles Ward at the beginning of 1892 by some forty-four of his ex-pupils,

Figure 1. Illuminated address presented to Charles Ward

alluding to their

appreciation on his many sterling qualities as a Gentleman and born teacher.

and their gratitude

for the thorough education and business training they received at his hands.

Accompanying the address is a large, framed and illuminated collection of portraits of some of these pupils, though unfortunately the subjects are not now identifiable – and there are also scenes in Darton; originally they had also been accompanied by a gold watch and chain. The principal coloured address was illuminated and scripted by George Shaw of Barnsley, whom the 1897 trade directory shows as a printer and stationer at No. 1, Peel Square; the names of the subscribers to the presentation include those of Burnley and Lodge, well known locally in that period as local colliery owners.

The Victorians were somewhat addicted to making presentations to local worthies, but the survival of these illustrations does raise the twin questions of who was Charles Ward, and what was Darton Grammar School? In fact, a Grammar School at Darton is referred to as existing in 1564, and under his will dated 1668 the school was endowed with the interest of £500 by George Beaumont of The Oaks in Darton, described as a Dantzig merchant. His endowments, of £1,000 in all – part being for other charitable purposes – were formalised by a deed of trust in 1675. The school was to be free to the children of the inhabitants of Darton ecclesiastical parish – an area larger than Darton itself – and taught by 'a good schoolmaster'. The school building existing by 1675 was rebuilt in or about 1800, but the children were taught only the so-called '3 Rs', although in the 1820s they were expected to be able to read the New Testament before being admitted; the endowment was invested in the purchase of farms at Keresforth Hill and Pogmoor. In the 1820s attendance averaged some 60 (less, it was commented, in harvest time) and in 1892 averaged 100; in 1866 there was one shilling (5p) entrance fee, with 41 boys and 32 girls.

During the Victorian period it was not uncommon for some of the anciently endowed village schools to take to themselves the title of grammar school: it betokened a certain standing and antiquity, although in the case of the schools at Normanton and Darton there were perhaps no – or at best short – periods when the classics were actually taught: demand was of course limited in that field, although at Ossett the name was adopted for the village school and classics were newly taught.

To this anciently-established school came in about 1857 as master Charles Ward, a young man then of about twenty-three, a native of Leeds, according to the census returns. He was neither a graduate nor a certificated (ie, trained) teacher, but he possessed a natural ability as a teacher and was highly regarded at Darton. He married a daughter of Thomas Thexton, some time his predecessor as Master of Darton Endowed School and subsequently Vicar of Darton until his death in 1854. Mrs Ward was assistant mistress in the school and his second wife, Elizabeth, was mistress there in 1897.

The fact that the farms close to Barnsley town which had been bought by the school's trustees had coal below them led in the early part of the second half of the nineteenth century to an increase in the trustees' income, and it was possible to rebuild the school premises in 1875.

Charles Ward remained as Master until retirement at the end of 1899, having held office for over forty years. There were then eighty-seven children on the school's register. Ward himself died early in 1905, in his early eighties.

Ward had provided a substantial education for his girls and boys, several of whom had 'got on' in life; and some had been taught book-keeping. Perhaps in a real sense the provision of a good education was inherited from Ward by the subsequent sending of boys from Darton to the grammar school at Wakefield, and inherited more locally by the establishment of the modern-day Darton High School.

Sources

Census returns, 1861
Endowed Charities Reports, West Riding, vol.V (1899).
P J Wallis and W E Tate, *A Register of Old Yorkshire Grammar Schools* (?1956).
West Riding Trade Directories.
Local History Study Centre, Wakefield: Chas Ward MSS, various MSS., card index.
Letter from C P Shaw, Darton, 1998.

CONTRIBUTORS

THE EDITOR
2. GLIMPSES OF MEDIEVAL BARNSLEY

Brian Elliott was born in Royston and spent his childhood in Carlton and Monk Bretton. He taught Geography for fourteen years at the secondary school in Royston where he was a departmental head and year tutor. From 1985, he worked as an Adult Education manager and lecturer at Rother Valley College, in the Rotherham area, retiring early from the post of Head of the School of General Education in 1999. His M Phil, from Sheffield University, was for research on Barnsley and its neighbourhood *c.*1660-*c.*1760. He now works mainly as a freelance writer, editor, and consultant, overseeing all *Aspects* titles for Wharncliffe Books and also their developing *Foul Deeds and Suspicious Deaths* series. Recent publications include *A Century of Barnsley* (Sutton/W H Smith, 2000); *Darfield & Wombwell* (2001, in Sutton's *Britain in Old Photographs* series, *Barnsley Pits and Pitmen* (Wharncliffe, 2001); and (as editor) *The Miners' Strike Day by Day* (Wharncliffe, 2002).

---

1. WHAT'S IN A NAME? THE ANCIENT PLACE-NAMES OF BARNSLEY METROPOLITAN BOROUGH

Melvyn Jones was born in Barnsley and educated at the Holgate Grammar School and the universities of Nottingham and Leeds. He taught for seven years at Myers Grove, Sheffield's first comprehensive school, and then for nine years at Sheffield City College of Education before its amalgamation into Sheffield City Polytechnic in 1976. He retired from the post of Head of Academic Resources in the School of Leisure and Food Management at Sheffield Hallam University in 1997. He is now Visiting Professor at the Centre for Environmental Conservation and Outdoor Leisure at Sheffield Hallam University. He has written extensively on the social and economic history of South Yorkshire. He is editor of *Aspects of Rotherham*, volumes 1-3 and *Aspects of Sheffield*, volumes 1-2. Recent publications include *The Making of the South Yorkshire Landscape* (Wharncliffe Books, 2000), *Protecting the Beautiful Frame* (Hallamshire Press, 2001), *In and Around Thorpe Hesley and Wentworth* (with Joan Jones, Tempus Publishing, 2001) and *Whitley Hall, an illustrated history* (with Joan Jones, Green Tree publications, 2002). Wearing another hat he is BBC Radio Sheffield's 'History Man' and has completed more than 150 live programmes. A book based on the radio programmes – *Glimpses of South Yorkshire's Past* – will be published next year.

3. MY WORKING LIFE AT NEEDHAM BROTHERS & BROWN OF BARNSLEY

Roy Portman was born in Barnsley where he has lived most of his life. Educated at Park Road Junior School, Mark Street Central and Barnsley Technical College, he started his apprenticeship at Needham Brothers & Brown, Pontefract Road, in 1937 and worked there for forty-three years, latterly as Foreman Pattern-Maker. He developed an interest in photography in about 1949 and joined Barnsley Photographic Society in 1952. Roy has won many competitions and awards in the Society's annual exhibition, once held in the Cooper Galleries. No longer an active member, he was elected Hon Vice President a few years ago. Roy has been a member of several local history groups and is an active member of the Barugh Green Local History Group where he often gives illustrated talks on the changing face of Barnsley, the history of photography etc. His large collection (*c.*3,000 prints and transparencies) of Barnsley has recently been donated to the Tasker Trust. A book, celebrating Roy's personal photographic archive and his interest in Barnsley's history, is planned for publication in 2003.

4. STATION TAXIS: MEMORIES OF A SMALL FAMILY BUSINESS IN BARNSLEY DURING THE 1950S AND EARLY 1960S.

Mike Stringer was born at Skiers Spring, Hoyland, in 1940. He attended Agnes Road School and Ardsley Oaks Secondary Modern. Twice whilst in his teens he was a long-term patient in Wath Wood Hospital, which he regards as having an important influence on his future life. For six months he was a student at Barnsley School of Art before leaving the area to live in London and the South East where he found work as a kitchen porter, a factory and fairground hand, a pavement artist and as verger for the Church of St Paul, Shadwell, in London's East End. He married Ray, a teacher, in 1968 and became an under-gardener for Lord Wraxall in Somerset. After living in Bedfordshire, Barnsley and Cambridgeshire, Mike and Ray moved to Billericay, Essex. They have two grown-up children, Megan and Tom. Mike now works as a freelance illustrator, specialising in wildlife subjects, designing and illustrating books, greeting cards and illustrating designs for pottery and other companies. He also makes hand-painted house signs which he sells through shops.

5. BORN IN BARNSLEY: RAISED IN SMITHIES

Colin Taylor, born in the Barnsley area in 1924, of parents who were Lancashire millworkers. He was educated at Burton Road Elementary School, Smithies and Barnsley Grammar School. In 1940 he left the sixth form to take up a post at David Brown's Foundry in Penistone, working as an analytical chemist. In the war he served in the RAF as a pilot and afterwards met his wife, Eileen, a WAAF in the met office, at Leeming Airfield, North Yorkshire. They married in 1947. The Taylors emigrated to Hamilton, Canada in 1954, moving to Buffalo, New York three years later and then on to San Francisco (1959) and Stockton, California (1968). Colin had become a General Manager in the foundry industry. The next move, in 1970, was to Oregon where he was President of a manufacturing company that served the foundry industry. Colin has continued to work as a consultant since retirement and hopes to publish a more detailed memoir of his life, particularly relating to his formative and unforgettable years in Barnsley.

6. POSTCARDS FROM BARNSLEY

Norman Ellis was born and raised in Outwood, near Wakefield. He was educated at the village's Ledger Lane Council School and Rothwell Grammar School. He worked for three years in Wakefield as an engineering draughtsman, before obtaining a similar post at an Ossett firm where he stayed for thirty-nine years. He has lived in Ossett since 1960. Norman took early retirement in 1989 to concentrate on his leisure  interests, the main one being local history. In addition to numerous articles, he has written almost twenty books, including titles on Wakefield, Dewsbury and the Spen Valley. Being especially interested in industry and transport, he has also produced studies on Yorkshire collieries and railway stations. Norman's writing relies heavily on old picture postcards which he has collected since 1970. Other interests include photography and gardening.

7. EDMUNDS AND SWAITHE MAIN COLLIERIES
12. CHARLES WARD, MASTER AT DARTON'S VICTORIAN GRAMMAR SCHOOL

John Goodchild, M Univ was born at Wakefield in 1935 and was involved in local history study from the age of about fifteen. He was

founder-curator of Cusworth Hall Museum and spent his last years employed as Principal Local Studies Officer and Archivist at Wakefield, retiring at the age of fifty-nine. Subsequently, he has spent some seven years in establishing his own unique Local History Study Centre at Wakefield (which receives some 2,000 users a year and is available by appointment, free of charge), lecturing, writing and researching, and leading guided tours. He has now produced well over 150 books and printed essays. He continues actively to collect books, manuscripts, maps and illustrations relating principally to the central West Riding. John was awarded an Honorary Master's Degree by the Open University 'for academic and scholarly distinction, and for public services.'

8. A SHORT LIFE AND A LONG DEATH: THE DEARNE DISTRICT LIGHT RAILWAYS

Richard Buckley was born in 1943 and spent most of his childhood in Devon. A love for transport was engendered, however, by visits to his grandparents in Liverpool, a city which in those days possessed such delights as streamlined trams and the Overhead Railway. A graduate of Hull University, he went on to gain an M.Sc. in Politics from Strathclyde University and a Ph.D. in Economic History, again from Hull. The latter was gained for a study of the decline of the tramway industry in South Yorkshire. He has spent most of his working life as a parish priest in Yorkshire. Currently he works for an overseas aid charity and is based in Sheffield. He and his wife Sylvia have three sons. Previous publications include – *A History of Tramways* and *Tramways & Light Railways of Switzerland & Austria,* plus a number of articles in academic and enthusiast journals.

9. EXTRACTS FROM ROYSTON SECONDARY SCHOOL LOG BOOKS, 1934-1945

John Broom was born in East Anglia, of Norfolk and Essex roots. Brought up in Hull, he attended Riley High School where his interest in History, particularly the local variety, was stimulated. After studying for a History Degree at the University of Sheffield, he spent a mundane year moving pieces of paper around the country for the Civil Service before a teacher-training course led to a post in the Humanities Department at Royston High School. Now in his ninth year at the school, he also works as an examiner in History and Leisure and Tourism, has produced educational material for museums and worked as a census enumerator in 2001. John's other interests include Local and Family History. Married with two small daughters, Rosie and Sophie, he is a keen local sportsman, playing cricket for Royston CC and running events from five miles up to marathons for Barnsley Athletics Club.

10. JOHNNY WESTON'S MONK BRETTON: A SOCIAL CHRONICLE OF A VILLAGE IN THE FIRST HALF OF THE TWENTIETH CENTURY

G B (Barry) Jackson was born in the old Monk Bretton Urban District in 1935 and was educated at Burton Road School and Barnsley Grammar School. After National Service in the RAF, he went up to Downing College, Cambridge where he graduated with Second Class Honours in History. He taught for twenty-seven years in the Barnsley area, mostly at Penistone Grammar School, where in addition to his History teaching, he was Head of Careers.

He took medical retirement in 1987 following a stroke. Barry was, in his younger days, an altar server (twelve years) and choir member (seven years) at Monk Bretton Church and played for Monk Bretton Cricket Club for twenty-one seasons. Since 1968 he has lived at Cawthorne, the home of the ancestors of his schoolteacher wife, Joan. During those thirty-four years he has held positions on the Parish Council and with the village Choral Society. He was Churchwarden for thirteen years, is the President and a trustee of Cawthorne Victoria Jubilee Museum, and in 1992 published for that building's benefit *Cawthorne 1790-1990; a South Yorkshire village remembers its past.* He and his wife have a married daughter who also read history at university.

11. MEMORIES OF CANON SORBY AND SOME CHARACTERS OF OLD DARFIELD

Margaret Mann, née Longden, was born in Darfield where she attended Shroggs Head Infants' School and Darfield Church of England School. Margaret continued her education at Barnsley Girls' High School and Lincoln Teacher Training College. She taught at Great Houghton County Primary and other West Riding schools and eventually at Worsbrough St Mary's. She was a founder member of the South Yorkshire Society for Autistic  Children, Secretary of Darfield Amenity Society and an active member of Darfield Dramatic Society. In 1964, Margaret published *Darfield Village and Church.* This is Margaret's second contribution to the *Aspects of Barnsley* series. Married with two grown-up children, she now lives in retirement in Cornwall.

Index of Places

(NB Street names are for Barnsley unless otherwise stated; inns/pub names are in italics)

Barnsley